The Future of
Canada Post Corporation

Report of the
Canada Post Mandate Review

Cat. Nº.   Po 10-1\1996E
ISBN   0-662-25048-6

Publié aussi en français sous le titre :
L'Avenir de la Société canadienne des postes

Government of
Canada

Gouvernement du
Canada

Canada Post
Mandate
Review

Examen
du mandat
de la Société
canadienne
des postes

350 Albert Street
4th Floor
Ottawa, Ontario
K1A 0S5

350, rue Albert
4ième étage
Ottawa (Ontario)
K1A 0S5

1-800-823-8373

July 31, 1996

The Honourable Diane Marleau
Minister Responsible for Canada Post Corporation
Room 256, Confederation Building
House of Commons
Ottawa, Ontario
K1A 0A6

Dear Madam Minister,

On November 6, 1995, your predecessor, the Honourable David
Dingwall, announced my appointment as Chairman of the Canada
Post Mandate Review. The Terms of Reference called for my
report to be submitted not later than July 31, 1996.

Accordingly, I today have the honour of submitting to you the
report of the Canada Post Mandate Review.

Sincerely yours,

George Radwanski
Chairman

Canada

Table of Contents

Introduction   i

1.   Overview   1

2.   **The Financial Position of Canada Post Corporation**   5

     2.1   Current Financial Position   5
        2.1.1   Profitability   5
        2.1.2   Cash Reserves   6
        2.1.3   Summary of Current Position   9

     2.2   Future Financial Prospects   10

     2.3   Financial Self-sufficiency   13
        2.3.1   Commercial Rate of Return   14
        2.3.2   Break-even   16

     2.4   Summary of Financial Position   18

3.   **Canada Post Corporation's Competitive Stance**   19

     3.1   Competition in Unaddressed Admail   24
        3.1.1   Conflict of Interest   26
        3.1.2   Mailbox Access   28
        3.1.3   Restrictions on Admail   30

     3.2   Competition in Courier Services   31
        3.2.1   Cross-subsidization   32
        3.2.2   Pricing and Marketing   33
        3.2.3   Appropriateness of Involvement in Courier Industry   36

     3.3   Competition with Mailing Centres   37

     3.4   The Issue of Cross-subsidization   40
        3.4.1   Direct/Explicit Cross-subsidization   41
        3.4.2   Indirect/Implicit Cross-subsidization   44
        3.4.3   Leveraging   46

     3.5   Summary of Competitive Stance   48

4.   **The Corporate Culture of Canada Post Corporation**   49

     4.1   From Public to Private Orientation   49

     4.2   Impact on Corporate Culture   52

5. The Strategic Focus of Canada Post Corporation   58

    5.1 Supplementing Revenues   58

    5.2 Anticipating Volume Declines   60

6. The Governance of Canada Post Corporation   62

7. Recommendations   65

    7.1 Universal Service at Uniform Rates   66

    7.2 Removing the Exclusive Privilege   68

    7.3 Establishing a Regulatory Framework   71

    7.4 Privatizing Canada Post   73

    7.5 Removing Canada Post from Competitive Activities   77
        7.5.1 The Canada Post Viewpoint   79
        7.5.2 Convergence with Sound Management Practice   81
        7.5.3 Convergence with the Government's Policy Direction   82
        7.5.4 Competitive Areas to be Vacated   84

    7.6 Costs of Withdrawing from Competitive Activities   87
        7.6.1 Initial Exit Costs   88
        7.6.2 Ongoing Contribution Losses and Costs   89

    7.7 Revenue Strategies   89
        7.7.1 Postage Rates   89
        7.7.2 Contribution from Courier Services   91
        7.7.3 Tax or Levy on Unaddressed Admail   94

    7.8 Labour Costs   95

    7.9 Net Financial Implications of Strategic Repositioning   99

    7.10 Financial Relationship with the Government   101

    7.11 Reinforced Federal Identity   103

    7.12 Rural Post Office Closings and Service Issues   104

    7.13 Provision of Access to Government Services   107

    7.14 Improving Mail Delivery, Speed and Reliability   110

    7.15 The Issue of Community Mailboxes   112

    7.16 Predictability in Dealing with Canada Post   114

    7.17 Process for Setting Exclusive Privilege Postal Rate   115

7.18 The Governance of Canada Post   116

8. Conclusion   121

8.1   Summary of Findings   122

8.2   Summary of Recommendations   124

Appendices: 131

Appendix A - Terms of Reference   133
Appendix B - List of Submissions   135
Appendix C - Public Meeting Schedule   141
Appendix D - Executive Summary of Decima Research Report   145

Introduction

In reviewing the mandate and assessing the future of an institution that touches as many lives as Canada Post Corporation, one cannot hope to entirely satisfy everyone. Interests legitimately diverge, and perspectives honestly differ.

What is essential is that every point of view be given a full and fair hearing, and that all available information be objectively and thoroughly. assessed. This the Review has made every attempt to do. In carrying out the responsibilities entrusted to me on behalf of the Government by the then Minister Responsible for Canada Post, the Honourable David Dingwall, in November 1995, I have been guided at all times by a determination that the processes of this Review must be as open, accessible, independent and even-handed as humanly possible.

To this end, the Review placed advertisements in 678 newspapers and sent letters to close to 1,000 potentially interested parties, inviting written submissions by the deadline of February 15, 1996. A total of 440 formal submissions and 1,084 letters were received, including petitions from municipalities with a total of 2,480 signatures. To ensure maximum public access, all formal submissions were posted by the Review on the internet. As well, 1,116 telephone calls about substantive issues pertaining to the Review were received from Canadians across the country. This constitutes evidence of a remarkably high level of current nation-wide interest in the role and activities of Canada Post. By way of comparison, the last review of the mandate of the corporation a decade ago received a total of 131 submissions, including letters.

Public meetings were held in March and April in six Canadian cities: Vancouver, Winnipeg, Montreal, Halifax, Toronto and Ottawa. Their purpose was to permit the Review to hear first-hand a representative cross-section of the organizations, companies and individuals who had made submissions and to explore their views through brief dialogue. Canada Post and the Canadian Union of Postal Workers (CUPW), at their respective requests, appeared before the Review in each of the cities. Time was also set aside at the end of each day for members of the general public to offer brief comments. A total of 111 presentations were heard in 14 days of public meetings, not including the representatives of Canada Post and the CUPW, who appeared at each location.

To ensure that a sampling of the ideas and concerns of Canadians in rural areas could be communicated as clearly as those of interested parties in urban centres, the Review supplemented the formal public meetings with town hall meetings in Witless Bay, (Newfoundland) and Iqaluit, (Northwest Territories). As well, focus groups were held in the remote locations of Bay Bulls, (Newfoundland), Unity, (Saskatchewan) and Iqaluit. Urban focus groups were also held in Montreal, Toronto, and Calgary. A total of 96 individuals participated in these focus groups. And, finally, nation-wide quantitative research with a total sample of 1500 was conducted for the Review by Decima Research.

In order to provide access to the best possible information, the Review also had informal meetings with appropriate individuals and organizations in the United States and Canada. In the United States, the Review met in Washington with Mr. Michael S. Coughlin, the U.S. Deputy Postmaster, and senior members of his staff, as well as with Mr. Dan Blair, Staff Director, Postal Service Subcommittee of the U.S. House of Representatives. In New York, the Review met with specialists on the impact of information technologies at Columbia University, and with a panel of experts kindly assembled by the Canadian Consul General in New York, Mr. George Haynal. Here in Canada, the Review held extensive individual discussions with the senior management of Canada Post, including members of the Board of Directors, and with the leadership of all the postal unions, particularly CUPW, as well as with CUPW representatives from across the country. The Review also met with the executives of all the Postal Service Customer Councils and with a range of other private sector stakeholders.

It is appropriate here to thank all the individuals and organizations who took the trouble to make their views known in the course of this consultation process, and particularly those who appeared in person before the Review. It was a very encouraging and uplifting experience to see so many Canadians, whatever their points of view, demonstrating their caring about the institutions of this country and stating their concerns and ideas lucidly, thoughtfully and often in a spirit of remarkable candor.

I was assisted in the organizational, research and analytical work of the Review by a small staff of extraordinarily gifted and dedicated professionals, many of them seconded from various Government departments, who accomplished remarkable work in the short time available. In the structure of this Review, arriving at findings and recommendations was the sole province of the Chairman rather than a committee, so the staff are innocent of any shortcomings in the final result. No one could have wanted a more helpful and supportive team for a project of this nature. My deepest thanks to them all.

Without intruding inappropriately on the traditional professional anonymity of the other public servants on the staff, I do want to acknowledge particularly the contributions of the three members of the Review's "management team".

Dona Vallières was responsible for all communications and stakeholder liaison, including designing and organizing the entire consultation process of submissions, public meetings, town hall meetings and focus groups, and for the editing and production of this final report. Her consummate tact, skills and professionalism were the key to the success of the Review's efforts.

Art Lamarche, as Executive Assistant, handled all aspects of administration and staff and research coordination with exemplary expertise and boundless energy. Without his wide-ranging help, it would have been impossible to accomplish so much work in the available time.

Professor Donald Savoie, as Senior Policy Advisor, brought to the Review an encyclopaedic knowledge of public policy and an unfailing capacity for invaluable insights. His advice opened numerous avenues of thought and helped avoid many pitfalls.

Appreciation is also due to the members of the Advisory Committee of senior representatives from the Treasury Board Secretariat/Department of Finance, Privy Council Office and Public Works and Government Services, who were supportive of the work of the Review without in any way attempting to influence its course or substance. I also wish to thank the officials from Public Works and Government Services who, on behalf of the Minister Responsible for Canada Post, ensured that the Review had all necessary resources.

George Radwanski

1 Overview

In the decade since the last mandate review of Canada Post Corporation, there have been major changes in the technological, economic and policy environments in which the corporation operates.

There have also been important changes in the corporation itself. Canada Post's earlier years were an attempt to strike a delicate balance between the competing demands of public service and commercial orientation that are a tension inherent in most Crown corporations. Over the past decade, Canada Post has increasingly come down squarely on the commercial side of the equation. In the process, its corporate culture has changed dramatically, as has the place it occupies in the private-sector economy.

These changes are only the latest step in the evolution of a public enterprise that predates Canada itself and that has played a crucial role in the development of our nation. The lineage of our postal service extends unbroken from the "coureurs de bois" transporting messages by canoe between settlements, to today's corporation that is Canada's 28th largest company in terms of unconsolidated revenues, and our country's fourth largest employer.

Canada Post's 18,547 retail points of contact make it by far the most widespread and visible federal presence in Canada. Its activities touch the lives of nearly every citizen and every business. Virtually all Canadians receive mail, and most of us still rely on it to one extent or another; for many in rural and remote areas in particular, it remains a vital lifeline. Despite the growing availability of other forms of communication, 84% of Canadians still check their mail every day.[1]

---

[1] Quantitative research conducted for the Review by Decima Research; June 1996.

Much of the change that has taken place at Canada Post constitutes significant progress. As well, the current management of the corporation has a strongly-held vision of its future, and pursues that vision with vigour and determination. This Review was also struck by the sophistication and thoughtfulness of the current labour union leadership, and by their apparent sincerity in wishing to serve the public good while advancing the interests of their membership. The improvement in labour-management relations, from a previous condition which can only be described as toxic, is in itself a major achievement for our postal system.

But change always carries a price, and the exceptionally rapid pace of both external and internal change in recent years has taken a substantial toll on the corporation. Externally, two developments are particularly noteworthy: the emergence of a much more active and dynamic private sector in several fields that were previously the preserve of Canada Post, and the development of a new and more tightly focussed view of the proper role for government and its entities within the economy. Both these developments have the effect of throwing into question the appropriateness of some of Canada Post's current activities. Internally, at the same time, major changes in corporate vision, strategy and culture - particularly since the mid-1980s - have blurred the corporation's public policy focus and given rise to serious problems in terms of both the corporation's results and the appropriateness of its behaviour.

> CHANGE ALWAYS CARRIES A PRICE, AND THE EXCEPTIONALLY RAPID PACE OF BOTH EXTERNAL AND INTERNAL CHANGE IN RECENT YEARS HAS TAKEN A SUBSTANTIAL TOLL ON THE CORPORATION.

The causes for concern identified by this Review include the following:

♦ Canada Post Corporation has lost a total of $1.517 billion since its creation in 1982 - including a net loss totalling $154 million in the supposedly more "profitable" period beginning with the 1988/89 fiscal year. Its plans for achieving future financial soundness are unconvincing.

♦ The corporation has created serious issues of fairness and appropriateness by "leveraging" the network it has built up through its government-granted lettermail monopoly and through past outlays of public funds to compete with private sector companies from a position of strength they cannot match.

♦ Canada Post has developed such a reputation as an over-aggressive, indeed vicious, competitor that a significant number of Canadians, particularly operators of small businesses, are quite literally afraid of it. Even some of Canada's largest businesses have told this Review, in confidence, that they are afraid to publicly criticize the corporation, for fear that it will use its monopoly position to retaliate.

♦ Canada Post's strategic vision makes highly questionable policy or economic sense. It's a vision that would require the corporation to spread its activities ever wider through the private-sector economy, farther and farther away from the basic reasons for its existence, in order to make up revenue shortfalls and anticipated (perhaps wrongly) lettermail volume declines.

♦ Though it invokes "universal service at an affordable price" as its core mission, Canada Post has lost sight of the focus on public service that is the fundamental reason for its existence.

♦ The corporation is not subject to any adequately effective accountability mechanisms. Neither the Minister responsible for Canada Post, nor any other branch of the Government, nor even the corporation's own Board of Directors has any way of providing the sustained supervision necessary to ensure that its priorities and behaviour are fully consistent with the public interest.

♦ Canada Post is operating under the constraints of a collective agreement whose provisions - particularly with regard to pay for time not worked, flexibility and job security - are completely out of line with the new realities of today's workplace. The financial consequences of these provisions pose a serious threat to the eventual viability of the corporation and hence to the future of *all* its employees.

These problems, and others, create a need to adapt to changing realities by refocussing the strategic vision of the corporation, so that it can most effectively serve Canadians in the new circumstances of the present and the future.

In identifying the need for such a strategic repositioning, this Review has been guided by three key priorities:

♦ ensuring that all Canadians get the best possible postal service at an affordable price;

♦ ensuring that the postal needs of Canadian businesses are well met;

♦ ensuring that the functioning of Canada Post is fully consistent with the policy and fiscal priorities of the Government of Canada.

From all three points of view, the need to refocus the corporation is urgent. It is a finding of this Review that the cumulative effect of internal and external changes in recent years has been to create within Canada Post a serious crisis of identity, behaviour, purpose and long-term financial viability. The seriousness of this crisis is not diminished by the fact that it has developed gradually and quietly, outside the sight of most Canadians whose experience has been limited to receiving and sending mail with one degree of satisfaction or another.

> THE CUMULATIVE EFFECT OF INTERNAL AND EXTERNAL CHANGES IN RECENT YEARS HAS BEEN TO CREATE WITHIN CANADA POST A SERIOUS CRISIS OF IDENTITY, BEHAVIOUR, PURPOSE AND LONG-TERM FINANCIAL VIABILITY.

The following sections of this report will detail these findings, outline a policy context, and suggest some remedies to ensure that Canada Post will be positioned to give our nation the postal service we are entitled to expect as we head toward the next century.

2 The Financial Position of Canada Post Corporation

2.1 Current Financial Position

2.1.1 Profitability

Canada Post Corporation has lost money in nine of its 14 full years of operation (Table 1). All the corporation's profits have been in the period beginning with the 1988/89 fiscal year. But even in this latter period of five years of profits and three years of losses, the only substantial profits were in 1988/89 and 1989/90. Since then, Canada Post has had three years of very small profits and three years of quite substantial losses.

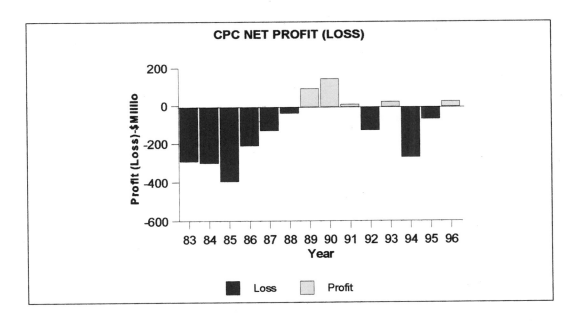

Year	83	84	85	86	87	88	89	90	91	92	93	94	95	96
Loss	-291	-300	-395	-210	-129	-38				-128		-270	-69	
Profit							96	149	14		26			28

Table 1

The profit Canada Post recently reported for the 1995/96 fiscal year is its first in the last three years. The corporation's reported net income of $28 million slightly exceeds its target of $26 million.

This profit was achieved, however, not by significantly improved performance but essentially as a result of a 2 cent stamp price increase effective August 1, 1995. The Review calculates that this increase provided $50 million in revenues. Were it not for the price increase, the corporation would likely yet again have shown a loss. A net income of $28 million on operating revenues of $4.9 billion can, in any event, scarcely be construed as a strong financial result.

The Review has noted that Canada Post describes its performance from 1988/89 to the present as "operating, in essence, at break-even level," and that it cites restructuring costs as a key explanation for the losses sustained.[2] Regrettably, this argument is unpersuasive. A loss is a loss, and the overall pattern of results does not lend itself to being viewed as one of breaking even. Rather, the corporation's chronic inability at least to consistently break even raises serious questions about the soundness of its business strategies.

2.1.2 Cash Reserves

Canada Post's cash and investment balances have fluctuated significantly over the years since its creation (Table 2). The corporation's cash and investments balance on April 1, 1982, was $172 million. This grew to $603 million as of March 31, 1988, largely due to the cash received from the Government to fund Canada Post's operating losses. The cash balances rose further, to $666 million in 1988/89 as Canada Post's first profit, proceeds from disposal of assets and long-term borrowings more than offset increased capital expenditures. Then the balances declined again, to a low of $218

---

[2]Canada Post Corporation, *Ensuring Universal Service at Affordable Rates* (Submission to the Review); February 15, 1996; page 25.

million[3] at March 31, 1994, due to the combined effects of losses from the 1992 strike, continuing capital expenditures, long-term investments and the payment of $66 million of dividends to the Government.

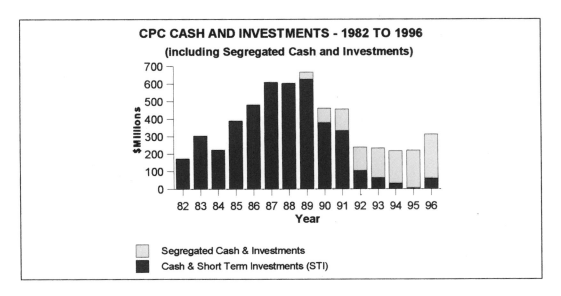

CPC CASH AND INVESTMENTS - 1982 TO 1996
(including Segregated Cash and Investments)

Year	82	83	84	85	86	87	88	89	90	91	92	93	94	95	96
Cash & STI	172	304	223	389	481	608	603	625	379	333	104	63	31	5	59
Segregated Cash & Investments				0	0	0	41	82	122	135	170	187	216	253

Table 2

A Coopers & Lybrand report, on which Canada Post relied heavily in its presentations to this Review, makes the following statement in assessing the current financial position of the corporation:

> "However, it has used its $600 million in cash reserves, $135 million in long term debt and long term leases to help finance needed investments. The company is now managing with an operating line of credit of $300 million that could be exhausted in 12

---

[3]This figure includes segregated cash and investments which the corporation has segregated for the purpose of managing cash flows relating to the employee termination benefits liability.

to 18 months if needed reinvestments continue and there is no improvement in profitability."[4]

Were that the case, Canada Post would effectively be broke. In the opinion of the Review, however, this does not present an entirely accurate picture. In 1988/89, after gaining access to its cash balances which were in the consolidated revenue fund, Canada Post decided to "segregate" some of its cash and short-term investments in order to manage the cash flows relating to its employee termination benefits liability. Up to March 31, 1996, the corporation has transferred $253 million of cash and short-term investments to segregated cash and investments.

Although it is management's intention to use segregated cash and investments for employee termination benefits, there is no legal barrier to using it for other purposes. In saying that the $600 million in cash reserves had been used up, the Coopers & Lybrand report was ignoring the segregated cash and investments of $216 million at March 30, 1995. That amount had increased to $253 million as of March 30, 1996.

Canada Post Corporation's cash and short-term investments, including segregated cash and investments, were $312 million at March 30, 1996.

Similarly, while Canada Post did draw on its $300 million short-term commercial paper line of credit in 1995/96 to meet seasonal borrowing needs, these short-term borrowings had been fully repaid by March 30, 1996. Particularly since the corporation has curtailed its capital expenditures, the Coopers & Lybrand statement that the line of credit could be exhausted in 12 to 18 months seems unduly pessimistic on the basis of currently available information.

---

[4]Coopers & Lybrand Consulting, *Choices for a Self-Sustaining Canada Post*, November, 1995; page 2.

2.1.3 Summary of Current Position

Canada Post has a dismal profitability record over nearly a decade and a half, accumulated losses of approximately $1.5 billion, a lack of retained earnings to service any future deficit years and a poor history of investment performance. Coupled with little evidence of control over costs, particularly labour, and an insistence on expanding rather than retrenching despite a difficult economic climate and poor performance, this would likely make Canada Post a company on the brink of disaster if it were in the private sector.

But since Canada Post is not a private sector corporation, its situation in reality is not directly comparable. Its borrowing is guaranteed by the Government, for instance, so it is not confronting queasy bankers. Its shares are not publicly traded, so it does not face market consequences for its performance. And, by the same token, it is subject to public policy constraints that deny it the relative freedom of manoeuvre a private sector company would have.

> THERE IS NO CONVINCING EVIDENCE THAT CANADA POST HAS TURNED THE CORNER FINANCIALLY, NOR THAT A CONTINUATION OF ITS PRESENT STRATEGIES AND PRIORITIES IS LIKELY TO PRODUCE MORE CONSISTENTLY SATISFACTORY RESULTS IN THE FUTURE THAN IT HAS IN THE PAST.

Under these circumstances, Canada Post Corporation is in no *immediate* financial danger. It remains able to fund its operations and to meet its obligations as they come due. But there is no convincing evidence that Canada Post has turned the corner financially, nor that a continuation of its present strategies and priorities is likely to produce more consistently satisfactory results in the future than it has in the past.

That, in turn, makes the corporation's medium-term future uncertain under a continuation of current approaches. Were its revenues to significantly decline, or its costs substantially to increase for several years for any reason, it is so precariously positioned that its financial viability could quite suddenly become at risk.

2.2 Future Financial Prospects

Canada Post's planned net income for 1996/97 is $107 million, an increase of $79 million over its most recent results - and by far the highest income since 1989/90, when the corporation made $149 million.

This dramatic increase in profitability is to be achieved primarily by higher revenue from operations, resulting from both pricing actions - namely, the continuing impact of the August, 1995 price increase, and increases in non-regulated prices - and planned business growth. Underlying the business growth projections is the assumption that Canada will have real Gross Domestic Product growth of 2.5% in 1996/97. In addition, Canada Post expects higher revenues from operations and on-going cost reduction and productivity initiatives to more than offset any cost increases.

The $107 million profitability target may well be achievable, but the corporation's past financial performance leaves no room for full confidence that it necessarily will be achieved. Key risks on the revenue side include such possibilities as a slowing in real GDP, failure to achieve planned business growth, and greater than anticipated volume losses due to price increases. As well, attempts to grow business volumes can actually be counter-productive unless the corporation has adequate product-costing systems to ensure that existing and new products and services make a sufficient contribution; Canada Post does not yet have a sufficiently effective system of this kind in place.

Similarly, planned reductions in operating costs could be imperilled by failure to realize full benefits of cost reduction and productivity initiatives, and by larger than anticipated cost increases. It is worth noting, in this regard, that Canada Post's recent Corporate Plans have referred to lower than expected productivity in discussing 1994/95 and 1995/96 results of operations.

Beyond the current fiscal year, Canada Post says it will achieve steadily increasing profits that will reach the $200-million mark before the turn of the century. There is no persuasive evidence that this anticipation is realistic on the basis of the corporation's current strategies.

These profitability goals are based on the corporation's intention of getting its cost of operations down to 95% of revenue. In pursuit of this target, the corporation has identified a number of possible key productivity and cost reduction initiatives for the period from 1997/98 to 2000/2001, some of which have not yet been approved by management or the Board of Directors. Nevertheless, the net benefits of these initiatives are still effectively included in the plan, under the rubric of unidentified productivity gains.

The problem is that many of Canada Post's major productivity and cost reduction initiatives require increased operational flexibilities, increased flexibility to downsize, and adjustments to benefit and wage structures - none of which are achievable under the current collective agreement with the Canadian Union of Postal Workers (CUPW). The corporation has tried unsuccessfully to obtain changes in this regard in past rounds of collective bargaining. There is no reason to assume, from the outset, that the normal course of events would produce a significantly different result in the contract negotiations that must take place in 1997. The financial plans do not take into account, on the other hand, either revenue losses that would result from any prolonged work stoppages or the costs that would be incurred if the corporation sought to achieve changes through large-scale buyouts.

> THE REVIEW NOTES, IN ASSESSING CANADA POST'S ANTICIPATIONS OF FUTURE PROFITABILITY, THAT THE CORPORATION HAS A CONSISTENT RECORD OF GREATLY OVER-ESTIMATING ITS FINANCIAL SUCCESSES A FEW YEARS INTO THE FUTURE.

In short, Canada Post's financial projections to the end of the century are based on major labour cost reductions that the corporation has outlined no coherent strategy for achieving. Without those cost reductions, even if all the other targets were achieved, under its current plans Canada Post would likely still be showing negligible - if any - profits by the year 2000.

The Review also notes, in assessing Canada Post's anticipations of future profitability, that the corporation has a consistent record of greatly over-estimating its financial successes a few years into the future (Table 3). Each Corporate Plan predicts that the ultimate profitability breakthrough is a few years away, then the projections steadily shrink in subsequent plans as the year in question approaches. The 1991/92 Corporate Plan, for instance, projected net income of $170 million for the 1994/95 fiscal year; the corporation's actual result in 1994/95 was a loss of $69 million. Similarly, the 1992/93 Corporate Plan, to cite the most recent example, projected net income of $200 million for 1995/96 - significantly more than the $28 million actually achieved. This reverse version of crying "Wolf!" takes an inevitable toll on credibility.

CPC CORPORATE PLAN FORECAST VERSUS ACTUAL NET INCOME ($MILLIONS)												
	89/90	90/91	91/92	92/93	93/94	94/95	95/96	96/97	97/98	98/99	99/00	00/01
Forecast												
1989/90 Plan	44	50	84	124	171							
1990/91 Plan		48	205	114	218	267						
1991/92 Plan			86	68	106	170	251					
1992/93 Plan				71	108	173	200	257				
1993/94 Plan					35	45	65	90	115			
1994/95 Plan						(47)	9	59	77	137		
1995/96 Plan							26	77	126	179	184	
1996/97 Plan								107	177	199	220	200
Actual	149	14	(128)	26	(270)	(69)	28					

Table 3

It is also noteworthy that, in its submission to this Review, Canada Post effectively endorses an analysis in the Coopers & Lybrand report of "CPC's financial prospects if it continued essentially as it is today". The Canada Post submission states:

> "In this model, CPC was assumed to continue to make productivity improvements at the level it has been in recent years and the continuation of other trends, including those with respect to rates and costs, was also assumed...The analysis indicates that CPC's current financial position cannot sustain it as a viable operation. Under this model, CPC would fall just short of break-even operating income over a 10-year period. Since this level in practice is likely to require annually about $100 million of

combined productivity gains and product contribution increases, even approximating break-even is hardly assured."[5]

For greater certainty, the Review asked Canada Post to clarify whether it was accepting these findings of the Coopers & Lybrand report as its own. The corporation responded that the report "...confirms our view that even if the current pace of improvements in rates, productivity and cost efficiencies could be maintained, this will not be sufficient to assure the long-term viability of the Corporation."[6]

Regrettably, the Review is unable to see - in either Canada Post's Corporate Plan or in its submission to the Review itself - any change in strategic direction far-reaching or coherent enough to make the Coopers & Lybrand scenario seem anything other than the most plausible one.

From all the available evidence, it is not possible to conclude with any confidence that Canada Post's financial performance in the years ahead will necessarily be substantially better than at present, if the corporation remains on its current strategic course. Improved profitability is not precluded. But the most likely outcome of doing more of the same is achieving more of the same results.

2.3 Financial Self-sufficiency

The Canada Post Corporation Act states, in Section 5(20) (b), that "The corporation in carrying out its objective, shall have regard to...the need to conduct its operations on a self-sustaining financial basis."

Neither the Act nor any regulation defines what is meant by "self-sustaining". The legislative mandate is consistent with any definition ranging from merely balancing the books, as was originally anticipated when the corporation was

---

[5]Canada Post Corporation, *Ensuring Universal Services at Affordable Rates,* op. cit.; pages 29-30.

[6]Letter from Henry J. Klassen, Vice-President Administration, Canada Post Corporation, to the Review; February 6, 1996.

created, to producing substantial profits, as the subsequent Progressive Conservative government ordered Canada Post to do.

2.3.1 Commercial Rate of Return

The April, 1989 federal budget, in particular, called on Canada Post to generate a commercial rate of return similar to that of large private sector companies in its field. The corporation continues to embrace that objective with considerable enthusiasm, and indeed argues vigorously for its retention in preference to other possible definitions of self-sustainability. In its submission to this Review, the corporation states:

> "The most practical reason for the maintenance of a commercial return objective is that achieving that return will enable CPC to improve service, maintain and extend its existing network as Canada's population grows, make additional investments that are likely to be required to enhance productivity and adjust its mix of services in relation to market developments."[7]

Curiously, Canada Post's enthusiasm for the commercial return objective is undiminished by the distance it remains from achieving it.

The corporation recently engaged RBC Dominion Securities to quantify the target ranges and benchmarks that would constitute appropriate commercial performance. By every standard, Canada Post's results to date fall dramatically short (Table 4).

---

[7]Canada Post Corporation, *Ensuring Universal Service at Affordable Rates*, op. cit.; page 40.

CPC FINANCIAL RATIOS		
	Target Ratios	**CPC Consolidated Ratios 1995/96**
Leverage		
Debt to equity	45 - 65%	27%
Cash flow to debt	40 - 45%	68%
Liquidity		
Current ratio	09 - 1.1	0.5
Gross interest coverage	4 - 6 times	1.8
Profitability		
Return on equity	12 - 14%	2.8%
Operating profit margin	4 - 6%	1.4%
Investment		
Capital asset investment rate	9 - 10%	2.4%
Cash flow to capital expenditures	80 - 90%	249.9%
Dividend payout ratio	30 - 40%	0%

Ratio Definitions:

Debt to equity	Total debt as a percentage of equity
Cash flow to debt	Operating cash flow as a percentage of long-term debt (including current portion)
Current ratio	Current assets divided by current liabilities
Gross interest coverage	Earnings before interest earned and expensed divided by interest expense
Return on Equity	Net income as a percentage of average equity
Operating profit margin	Income from operations as a percentage of revenue from operations
Capital asset investment rate	Net capital asset investment as a percentage of average gross capital assets
Cash flow to capital expenditure	Operating cash flow as a percentage of net capital expenditures
Dividend payout ratio	Dividends as a percentage of net income

Table 4   **(Review calculations)**

In its submission to the Review, the corporation itself acknowledges:

"Applying these ratios and ranges to the financial results of CPC... CPC fails to meet almost all the targets, including those relating to profitability, and in many cases by considerable margins."[8]

According to the Coopers & Lybrand Consulting report commissioned by Canada Post, attaining "self-sufficiency" on the basis of a commercial rate of return would require the corporation to achieve a

---

[8]Ibid., page 42.

net income from operations of between $100 million and $170 million a year.[9]   Analysis by the Review indicates that the Coopers & Lybrand report includes termination benefits as long-term debt and calculates interest on this item.   This appears to be overly conservative. The savings gained by removing these items reduce the net income Canada Post would need under this scenario of self-sufficiency to the range of $90 million-$150 million a year - still a long way from this year's $28 million.

2.3.2 Break-even

But achievement of commercial rates of return is not the only possible model of self-sufficiency that can be contemplated for Canada Post, given its status as a Crown corporation. The corporation could also be self-sufficient on a break-even basis, provided that breaking even is correctly defined to include meeting all its appropriate financial needs.

Broadly speaking, a company must meet certain requirements in order to be considered healthy. These requirements include:

♦ ability to meet its operating costs;
♦ ability to meet its debt obligations;
♦ ability to invest in capital equipment as needed;
♦ ability to access the debt markets, as needed, in order to make investments to sustain its business.

These requirements apply to all companies, whether in the private or the public sector, regardless of the operating scheme they employ. Beyond that, the essential difference between companies operating on the basis of commercial rate of return or break-even is whether or not the company pays out profits to shareholders as a return on their investment.

---

[9]Coopers & Lybrand Consulting, *Choices for a Self-Sustaining Canada Post*, op.cit.; page 3. (The report refers to "net income from operations, before interest and taxes, of between $250 and $350 million per year." For reasons of clarity, this has been converted here to net income).

In the case of Canada Post, the corporation is currently able to meet its operating costs and its debt obligations. Its ability to invest in capital equipment is constrained, however, and its leverage and liquidity ratios would prevent it from accessing additional borrowing on the open market on the basis of commercial criteria.

Canada Post's needs for investment in capital assets in the years ahead are not necessarily huge. The corporation has increasingly been moving toward leasing as an alternative to purchasing. As well, some of the expenditures included in Canada Post's capital budget are for electronic products that are not part of the current network and that are therefore not required to maintain or expand the existing physical infrastructure.

> THE REVIEW ESTIMATES THAT, UNDER THIS EXPANDED DEFINITION OF BREAK-EVEN, CANADA POST'S NET INCOME WOULD HAVE TO BE IN THE RANGE OF $70-100 MILLION A YEAR.

If the only *operating* reason for Canada Post to pursue a commercial rate of return is the goal of being able to borrow on the open market, it should be noted that there is an alternative: the Government could continue to guarantee the corporation's borrowings from the private markets, on condition that the corporation must meet certain public policy and performance objectives.

Under such a scenario, it would still be essential for Canada Post to have sufficient earnings to fund necessary capital expenditures and normal expansion of the core business, and to set aside sufficient reserves to insulate against years when there might be unanticipated earning shortfalls. This goes beyond the generally accepted concept of break-even, where revenues roughly equal expenses. The Review estimates that, under this expanded definition of break-even, Canada Post's net income would have to be in the range of $70-100 million a year.

2.4 Summary of Financial Position

On the basis of the above considerations, the Review has reached the following conclusions about the current and anticipated future financial position of Canada Post Corporation:

> FINDING #1: Canada Post Corporation is in no immediate financial danger. But its performance falls far short not only of a commercial rate of return, but also of an acceptable definition of breaking even. There is no basis for confidence that a continuation of the corporation's current strategic direction will produce sufficiently improved results in future years. Consequently, the current course imperils Canada Post's longer-term financial viability.

3 Canada Post Corporation's Competitive Stance

Canada's postal service has been involved in competitive activity, in one sense or another, since its earliest days. The mail has competed over the years with the telegraph, the telephone, the teletype, faxes, electronic mail and other forms of technology for share of the total communications market. The post office has also historically provided various services which competitively overlapped to some degree with private businesses. As Canada Post points out:

> "Canadian postal administrations have, for example, been providing parcel services since 1859, unaddressed printed matter distribution services (such as flyers) since 1903, expedited delivery of documents since 1914, courier services since 1979, and 'hybrid' hardcopy services since 1972."[10]

The nature, extent and intensity of the postal involvement in competition have changed fundamentally, however, since the creation of Canada Post as a Crown corporation. The change has been particularly marked in the years since 1986, when the Government of the day urgently ordered the corporation not only to balance its books but to start achieving commercial rates of profitability. Since then, competitive ventures have been central to Canada Post's business strategy. The corporation insists that it

> THE NATURE, EXTENT AND INTENSITY OF THE POSTAL INVOLVEMENT IN COMPETITION HAVE CHANGED FUNDAMENTALLY SINCE THE CREATION OF CANADA POST AS A CROWN CORPORATION.

can afford to provide universal postal service at uniform rates only if it "leverages" its existing network by maximizing revenues through as many additional businesses as possible.

---

[10]Canada Post Corporation, *Ensuring Universal Services at Affordable Rates,* op.cit.; pages 10-11.

Previous competitive activities were either *defensive*, intended primarily to protect the core lettermail service from rival means of communication, or *ancillary* to that core service. Today's Canada Post, in contrast, has stepped quite aggressively into the private sector with the aim of carving out new sources of business and revenues. The corporation has launched competitive initiatives in such fields as unaddressed admail, the courier industry - including the purchase of Purolator Courier in 1993 - business support services, and even desktop publishing and instances of retail sale of such items as greeting cards and office supplies.

This has created a serious anomaly: an unregulated public sector monopoly engaged in unrestrained competition with the private sector.

Postal services in most other countries have a monopoly, or exclusive privilege, over core lettermail services, and they also compete with the private sector to one extent or another. But there are usually safeguards to mitigate that competition. In the United States, for instance, the Postal Rates Commission consistently exerts downward pressure on the U.S. Postal Service's monopoly prices and upward pressure on the non-monopoly ones. The British Post Office has rigid structural separation between its various types of operations. In European countries, there is a movement towards "unbundling" under which competitors can use parts of a postal service's network at the same prices it charges itself, effectively precluding competitively unfair pricing.

> THIS HAS CREATED A SERIOUS ANOMALY: AN UNREGULATED PUBLIC SECTOR MONOPOLY ENGAGED IN UNRESTRAINED COMPETITION WITH THE PRIVATE SECTOR.

In virtually any conceivable scenario, the behaviour of such an entity as Canada Post would be perceived as unfair by those adversely affected by it. Each element of the situation guarantees such a perception. The power and financial resources of the state pitted against individual companies, particularly small businesses, can scarcely avoid seeming disproportionate. The use of a monopoly position in one field as a foundation for competitive activity in other fields, whether closely related or not, inevitably invites suspicions of cross-subsidy and other forms of undue advantage. And the absence of regulation, or any other meaningful supervision, precludes the possibility of any reassurance that excesses are not being committed.

The problem is compounded by Canada Post's own particular competitive style. Despite the understandable concerns that a corporation in its unique position might be using revenues from its monopoly to cross-subsidize unfairly low prices for its competitive activities, Canada Post invokes "commercial sensitivity" in refusing to publicly release detailed cost and profit information for its various products and services. Aggrieved competitors would be unlikely to be fully satisfied by assurances from any third party - however independent - as to an absence of cross-subsidy, without being able to judge for themselves.

Even worse, Canada Post itself still does not *have* accounting systems that identify the actual costs and revenues of each specific product and service with satisfactory precision, despite having been urged repeatedly over the past decade to put such systems into place. Instead, the corporation uses an approach technically known as the "regulatory method" to prepare its Annual Cost Study. This method consists of allocating variable and specific fixed costs to each product line, but leaving common fixed costs unallocated because the corporation says they would remain unchanged if any one product or product group were removed. Roughly 40% of total costs are unallocated.

The Review has noted that Canada Post regularly engages independent experts to certify that its accounting and costing methodology within the Annual Cost Study is appropriate and reasonable. But it does not necessarily follow that the Annual Cost Study approach itself can satisfactorily answer all the questions that arise, nor that what is appropriate and reasonable from the standpoint of accountants and economists is sufficient in *public policy* terms in the case of a public sector monopoly engaged in aggressive private sector competition.

In essence, Canada Post's premise is that it has a collection, sorting, transportation and distribution network whose costs are virtually immutable, and that therefore only the "extra" costs of providing any given competitive product or service are real costs that can be allocated. These products and services, consequently, don't show a profit or loss in the parlance of the corporation; they make a "contribution" toward the fixed costs. The fundamental flaw of this approach is that it inherently involves subjective - and potentially inaccurate or self-serving - judgments as to what can or cannot be allocated, and therefore as to what price must be charged for a given product or service to reflect its true cost and avoid cross-subsidization.

The anomaly of an unregulated public sector monopoly corporation in unrestrained competition with the private sector is therefore intensified by a second anomaly: that corporation carries out its competitive activities on the basis of cost-accounting processes that are neither publicly open, transparent, reliable nor in any possible way confidence-inspiring.

The consequences are entirely predictable:

> "I find it very frustrating to have my own government as my worst competitor. I use 'worst' in the worst sense of that word. Canada Post has a serious conflict of interest. It is a service provider to weekly newspapers. We have no choice for a substantial part of our delivery...Yet it wants to compete with us, and competes with us in a quite unfair manner."
>> Bob Verdun, Editor & Owner
>> The Elmira Independent newspaper, Elmira, Ont.

> "In 1990 I operated a company that distributed flyers in Woodstock, Moncton, Fredericton and St. John in New Brunswick, and Amherst in Nova Scotia. This distribution company is now closed, and I had to lay off over 750 carriers and 7 full-time staff...I lost most of my business to Canada Post, a Crown corporation run by the Government of Canada, Yes, my own government ended up putting me out of business, and not the private sector."
>> Gary Winsor, Owner & Operator
>> Budget Flyer Delivery, Bathurst, N.B.

> "Mowat Express has been in business for 43 years operating throughout Ontario and Quebec. In that time we have grown, we have prospered, and we have competed successfully against United Parcel Service, Federal Express, the previously-independent Purolator, and many others...But since the acquisition of Purolator by Canada Post, there has been a substantial and negative change in our marketplace...I want to say that Canada Post has damaged my business. I believe it has done so deliberately. It has stolen our profits and it has tried to destroy our viability."
>> John Mowat, President & CEO
>> Mowat Express, Toronto, Ont.

Setting aside for the moment the objective validity of the perceptions expressed, the Review finds that there is serious cause for concern in the fact itself that people who give every appearance of being decent, hard-working Canadians feel so unfairly treated by an entity of their own Government. The three individuals quoted above are representative of a significant number who spoke at the public meetings of the Review to express their anger and dismay at the perceived attempts of Canada Post to undermine their businesses. Others made similar points in written submissions, or through their industry associations. In all, the Review received a total of over 100 submissions complaining of unfair competition on the part of the corporation.

Canada Post emphatically dismisses such complaints. The corporation states in its submission to this Review:

> "As CPC broadened and improved the range of its services and tailored them to customer needs, CPC's competitors reacted not only in the marketplace, but also by persistently complaining that CPC improperly cross-subsidized its competitive services with revenues from services protected by the exclusive privilege. Styling themselves as the Coalition for Canada Post Accountability (formerly the Coalition of Canada Post Competitors), since 1989 this group of courier and parcels companies and newspapers has made these complaints before a range of public bodies in a manner intended both to downplay its members' obvious self-interest and the leading role in their affairs assumed by foreign-based multinationals such as UPS and FedEx."[11]

Such references to self-interest, corporate size or national origin do not, in the opinion of the Review, conclusively dispose of the issues in question. The legitimate self-interest of small Canadian businesses - the largest source of employment growth in our nation's economy - is not automatically inconsistent with the broad public interest. And large corporations, whether Canadian- or foreign-owned, are no less entitled to fair and appropriate treatment at the hands of any entity of the Government of Canada.

The concerns expressed about the nature and quality of Canada Post's competitive activities are serious, substantive and worthy of consideration on their merits.

---

[11]Canada Post Corporation, *Ensuring Universal Service at Affordable Rates*, op. cit.; pages 21-22.

Those concerns are primarily focused on three areas: unaddressed admail, courier services, and mailing centres. Each will be briefly examined in turn, along with a detailed examination of the issue of cross-subsidization.

3.1 Competition in Unaddressed Admail

Canada Post has increased its annual volume of unaddressed admail from 1.8 million pieces in the 1987/88 fiscal year to 4.8 million pieces in 1995/96 - an increase of 168%. This increase appears to have been brought about by a number of aggressive strategies dating back to 1989, when the corporation's unaddressed admail activities were "deregulated" so that it no longer had to publish proposed rate changes in the Canada Gazette for comment or submit them for Order-in-Council approval. This enabled Canada Post to develop new and flexible rate structures, including dramatic volume discounts. The corporation also established a new work force, separate from its letter carriers, to deliver "economy" unaddressed admail at particularly low rates, in addition to the admail delivered by letter carriers on their usual routes.

> THE CANADIAN NEWSPAPER INDUSTRY COMPLAINS THAT CANADA POST'S GROWTH IN ADMAIL HAS COME AT THE EXPENSE OF NEWSPAPER ADVERTISING REVENUES AND HAS BEEN ACCOMPLISHED BY UNFAIR COMPETITIVE METHODS.

The Canadian newspaper industry complains that Canada Post's growth in admail has come at the expense of newspaper advertising revenues and has been accomplished by unfair competitive methods. Community newspapers, in particular, have told the Review that the corporation's activities in unaddressed admail are threatening their very existence by luring away their revenues from advertising inserts which are crucial to their financial viability. The review received a total of 88 written submissions from community newspapers across Canada, in addition to the collective submission through their industry association. Other private sector distributors of unaddressed admail also complain that Canada Post competes unfairly.

There is no question that Canada Post, for its part, regards the newspapers as major competitors. In its submission to the Review, the corporation states:

"Intense competition in the unaddressed advertising distribution market includes private distributors and newspapers. The newspaper industry is attempting to establish national networks for advertising distribution among associated newspapers, thereby leveraging further the distribution networks they have established to deliver their core newspaper products."[12]

The view of the newspaper industry - both large urban dailies and community newspapers - and of other private sector distributors is that Canada Post's competition with them through its unaddressed admail activities is unfair in a number of key respects:

♦   They allege that cross-subsidization from monopoly lettermail revenues is enabling the corporation to charge unreasonably low prices for its unaddressed admail.

♦   The community newspapers, in particular, believe that Canada Post has a fundamental conflict of interest in functioning simultaneously as an essential monopoly service on which they must rely for distribution of their publications, and as a competitor fighting with them for advertising revenues. They allege that this leads the corporation to advantage admail over newspapers in a number of ways.

♦   The corporation's competitors believe that Canada Post derives unfair advantage from the fact that only it has access to locked apartment mailboxes and to community mailboxes for the distribution of admail.

♦   Competitors - as well as members of the public - complain that Canada Post is unfairly able to reach more households than other distributors by using its status as a federal Crown corporation to bypass municipal bylaws restricting delivery of junk mail.

---

[12]Canada Post Corporation, *Ensuring Universal Service at Affordable Rates*, op. cit.; page 19.

3.1.1 Conflict of Interest

Of the 669 community newspapers represented by the Canadian Community Newspapers Association, the Review was told, 519 are rural and therefore dependent in whole or in part on Canada Post for the distribution of their product. The same is true for the 49 rural newspapers among the total of 131 represented by Les Hebdos du Quebec. Thus a total of 568 community newspapers - the bulk of the Canadian community newspaper industry - currently find themselves in the position of simultaneously being highly dependent customers of Canada Post and also competitive targets of the corporation.

In their submissions to this Review, many community newspapers have complained that Canada Post in fact uses its monopoly power over their distribution to disadvantage them competitively. They allege that the corporation does this in two ways: by giving insufficient priority to delivering the newspapers on time, thus causing problems with their advertisers and customers, and by imposing rules that hamper their ability to offer advertising inserts within their own publications.

There is considerable evidence that community newspapers are often not delivered in a timely fashion by Canada Post. A connection between this unreliable postal delivery and Canada Post's competitive self-interest is only inferential, not proven. The corporation certainly puts itself in a difficult position as a service provider, however, when any improvement in the delivery of its main competitors for advertising flyers might hurt its own admail business.

> THE CORPORATION CERTAINLY PUTS ITSELF IN A DIFFICULT POSITION AS A SERVICE PROVIDER WHEN ANY IMPROVEMENT IN THE DELIVERY OF ITS MAIN COMPETITORS FOR ADVERTISING FLYERS MIGHT HURT ITS OWN ADMAIL BUSINESS.

There is also considerable anecdotal evidence that unaddressed admail is sometimes given priority over newspapers and other forms of mail in the postal process. This gains credence from the fact that

Canada Post's admail contracts are frequently based on specific delivery commitments. As one submission to the Review put it:

> "Our own newspapers have had trouble in this regard. At one post office in particular, our Monday papers were thrown in a corner and delivery was refused to customers, even though the customers asked for their papers at the wicket, until employees finished distributing Canada Post's flyers."[13]

Canada Post also imposes a number of requirements on newspapers that are to be mailed, with regard to advertising inserts, that have the effect, if not indeed the intent, of making such inserts less financially competitive.

The competitive activities of Canada Post in the admail field have had a seriously detrimental effect on the revenue base, and hence potentially the viability, of Canadian community newspapers. The Canadian Community Newspapers Association has told the Review that "recent insert revenue losses have, depending upon the size of the paper, ranged anywhere from $20,000 to $450,000 annually."[14] Individual submissions certainly substantiate that the financial damage has been real and significant. The Review is persuaded that the situation is serious enough to present a substantial threat to the future of this important sector of the Canadian economy and, even more significantly, of our national communications mix.

Whether various Canada Post practices are deliberately intended to competitively disadvantage community newspapers, or merely have that effect serendipitously from the corporation's point of view, is ultimately beside the point.

The reason for Canada Post's existence is to deliver the mail. Community newspapers - like other businesses and individuals - are dependent on it in that capacity. Being dependent on the services of

---

[13]Lighthouse Publishing Limited, Nova Scotia; **Submission to the Review.**

[14]Canadian Community Newspapers Association, **Submission to the Review,** op.cit.; page 22.

a powerful public sector monopoly, and simultaneously being at its mercy in its other capacity as an unrestrained competitor, is an intolerable position for anyone to be in. It is therefore a finding of the Review that Canada Post's current competitive activities in the unaddressed admail field constitute an intrinsic conflict of interest in its dealings with community newspapers.

3.1.2 Mailbox Access

Canada Post has exclusive control over the keys needed to access apartment building mailboxes for delivery purposes. The corporation obviously needs such access to all mailboxes in order to be able to deliver the mail. But in using this exclusive access - for its letter carriers and for its separate admail delivery force - to deliver unaddressed admail as well, Canada Post enjoys a competitive advantage not available to anyone else.

The Canadian Daily Newspaper Association argues in its submission to the Review:

> "Apartment coverage is often a critical issue for flyer advertisers, particularly in urban areas where there is a high concentration of apartment dwellings. In selecting a distribution vehicle, these advertisers will place considerable emphasis on whether they can get full coverage of apartments. That is something, however, that only Canada Post can offer, not by dint of its own efforts or business acumen, but because it is using the mailbox keys given to it by law for one purpose to achieve a totally different purpose, namely to secure a competitive advantage in this unregulated area of its business."[15]

Canada Post has responded to the Review that the Canadian Daily Newspaper Association took it to court on this issue, and that the Federal Court "rejected arguments that CPC had misused its statutory powers in permitting this access, concluding that 'no evidence (was found) that Canada Post was motivated by desire to shut out the

---

[15]Canadian Daily Newspaper Association, **Submission to the Review,** op.cit.; page 7.

competitors by using its exclusive control over apartment mailbox keys'."[16]

This does not, however, suffice to conclusively dispose of the issue. The Review notes that Mr. Justice Cullen rejected the case on the *legal* grounds that the corporation has not exceeded its parliamentary mandate by delivering admail to apartments, nor has it engaged in legally improper activity. Whether or not that parliamentary mandate should be modified in any respect, remains within the purview of this Mandate Review. Indeed, the Review notes that Mr. Justice Cullen in his judgment went on to say: "Establishing the parameters for the delivery of flyers by Canada Post and pricing is a task for Parliament. It is not for this Court to make legislation."[17]

> AGGRESSIVE COMPETITION MUST ALSO BE FAIR COMPETITION, PARTICULARLY WHEN IT IS CARRIED OUT BY AN ENTITY OF THE GOVERNMENT OF CANADA.

The key issue here, accordingly, is not legality, but fairness. This appears to the Review to be a clear instance where a distortion is created by applying to competitive commercial purposes the unrivalled market power and privilege that Canada Post derives from its public sector monopoly position.

Canada Post is aggressively competitive in the unaddressed admail field. But aggressive competition must also be fair competition, particularly when it is carried out by an entity of the Government of Canada. It is a finding of this Review that its exclusive access to apartment mailboxes for the delivery of unaddressed admail constitutes an unfair competitive advantage for Canada Post over the private sector.

---

[16]Canada Post Corporation, *Ensuring Universal Service at Affordable Rates: Testing the Requirements for the Mandate of Canada Post Corporation*; June 12, 1996; page 16.

[17]Reported at[1995]3 F.C.131; page 149.

3.1.3 Restrictions on Admail

It was brought repeatedly to the attention of the Review that Canada Post declines to comply with municipal by-laws that permit consumers to refuse the delivery of unaddressed advertising materials, better known in this context as "junk mail". The corporation instead invokes its immunity as a federal Crown agent.

Individuals have also complained of being told by Canada Post that if they refuse unaddressed admail, they won't receive delivery of any mail at all.

Canada Post argues that it is required by law to deliver all mail, and cannot permit recipients to pick and choose what they will accept. This argument is not altogether persuasive in view of the deregulated, commercial nature of admail and the fact that, by definition, it has no specific addressee. If people can refuse - by virtue of municipal bylaws - unaddressed admail delivered by private contractors, why should they be unable to refuse identical materials delivered by Canada Post? The purpose of a national postal service, surely, is not to compel acceptance of unwanted materials. It is also noteworthy that Canada Post has never asked Parliament or the Government for exemption from its perceived "obligation" to deliver unaddressed admail to unwilling recipients.

> INDIVIDUALS HAVE ALSO COMPLAINED OF BEING TOLD BY CANADA POST THAT IF THEY REFUSE UNADDRESSED ADMAIL, THEY WON'T RECEIVE DELIVERY OF ANY MAIL AT ALL.

The corporation has also responded that its unwillingness to comply voluntarily with municipal by-laws or the wishes of individual consumers is based on its preferring to wait for "an industry-wide solution". Two observations seem appropriate: first, despite being by far the largest purveyor of unaddressed admail, Canada Post has shown no apparent interest in providing leadership in search of such an industry-wide solution. Second, in municipalities where private-sector distributors are willing to comply with by-laws, it is unclear why Canada Post believes a partial, locally-based solution is inferior to no solution at all.

The issue is an important one for environmental, social and competitive reasons. From an environmental perspective, the sheer volume of unaddressed admail - much of it delivered by Canada Post, much of it never read - poses serious problems of waste of resources, litter, and disposal requirements through recycling facilities or landfill sites. From a social point of view, significant numbers of people have made clear that they find it invasive to be inundated - particularly by an entity of their own Government - with materials they do not want and are powerless to refuse.

In terms of competition, finally, Canada Post's refusal to comply with municipal by-laws restricting unaddressed admail gives it an unfair advantage over private-sector competitors. It is able to offer advertisers total coverage of all addresses, while others who must respect the by-laws, cannot. This is yet another instance where a distortion is created by Canada Post's presence, as a public sector entity with accordingly special privileges, in aggressive private-sector competition.

3.2 Competition in Courier Services

The courier industry in Canada began to grow in earnest in the years after 1967, when postal workers obtained the right to strike and postal users worried increasingly about availability and reliability of service. In 1979, having by then lost as much as 10% of its revenues to private couriers, Canada Post entered the courier field itself through the creation of Priority Post.

WITH THE PURCHASE OF PUROLATOR COURIER, CANADA POST BECAME BY FAR THE LARGEST PLAYER IN THE CANADIAN COURIER INDUSTRY.

The corporation's involvement in the Canadian courier industry remained relatively modest until its acquisition of Purolator Courier in 1993, however. With that purchase, Canada Post became by far the largest player. Its combined activities account for between 30% and 50% of the total courier market, depending on what definition is used for that market. Even if one accepts Canada Post's contention that the most relevant indicator is revenue share of the small parcel express market in Canada and that its share of that market is roughly 30%, that would still make the corporation by far the most powerful force in the Canadian courier industry, with a market share nearly three times that of its nearest rival.

Large multinational courier companies, small Canadian-owned courier companies and even, surprisingly, representatives of large users of courier services have complained with great vigour to the Review about Canada Post's augmented and highly competitive activities in this field.

The complaints fall into three broad categories of allegations:

◆ that Canada Post must be cross-subsidizing Purolator and Priority Courier with revenues from its lettermail monopoly;

◆ that Canada Post engages in unfairly aggressive pricing and sales techniques for its courier services;

◆ that Canada Post should not be in the courier field in any event, because it is well served by the private sector.

3.2.1 Cross-subsidization

As in the case of unaddressed admail, none of those alleging cross-subsidization purport to be able to offer concrete evidence, since they have no access to the corporation's books. Rather, their arguments are inferential and circumstantial.

In the case of Purolator, the point was repeatedly made to the Review that it is difficult to understand how the previously unprofitable company could in a short period of time raise the wages of its employees to bring them closer to those of Canada Post workers, invest in new equipment and expensive storefronts, increase expenditures on advertising, *and* lower its prices - and still be profitable for Canada Post. It may be that Canada Post has been reaping the benefits of changes made by the previous owner prior to the sale, but competitors remain unconvinced.

With regard to Priority Courier, competitors are convinced that the service must benefit from access to the Canada Post network to a far greater extent than the corporation admits. For instance, Randy Jackson, Vice-President of Lynden Air Freight, claimed to the Review at the public meeting in Vancouver that Canada Post frequently combines Priority Courier shipments with regular mail on scheduled airline flights to northern destinations. This gives Priority Courier an unfair advantage over competitors like his company, he argued, because its shipments benefit from the preferential treatment and pricing that is supposed to be reserved for Canada Post's exclusive-privilege mail.

In the category of circumstantial evidence, several submissions have pointed out a noteworthy convergence of events in 1994. That year, Canada Post announced its intention to raise the basic postage rate by 2 cents, from 43 to 45 cents, effective October 1. In August, the corporation informed its customers of a set of pricing changes - notably including price reductions in key market areas - for Priority Courier, Xpresspost and Regular Post, also effective October 1. At the end of September, the federal Cabinet rejected the proposed 2-cent increase in the postal rate. On September 30, Canada Post urgently informed its customers that the announced rate changes for Priority Courier, Xpresspost and Regular Post were cancelled.

Since these rates were not subject to Cabinet approval, the sequence of events is suggestive to some of Canada Post's competitors of a linkage between revenues from the corporation's monopoly lettermail business and the pricing of courier services - a linkage that should not exist in the absence of cross-subsidy. It suffices to observe here that coincidences like this, at the hands of a corporation that has long been accused of cross-subsidization, do nothing to allay suspicions.

The general issue of cross-subsidization will be addressed in greater detail in a subsequent section. It is appropriate to note at this point, however, that the submissions of concerned parties including Federal Express (FedEx), United Parcel Service (UPS) and the Canadian Courier Association have made what the Review considers to be an important point: whether or not Canada Post is actually engaged in cross-subsidization at present, there is a lack of transparent, effective safeguards to provide meaningful *assurance* that it is not doing so and that it will not do so in the future.

3.2.2 Pricing and Marketing

Canada Post's courier operations have been described as aggressive price leaders, and the evidence supports this view. As of mid-July, for instance, the quoted prices for overnight delivery of an envelope from Ottawa to Toronto or Montreal were: Priority Post $8.45; Purolator $9.95; UPS $11.00; FedEx $11.25. For overnight delivery of an envelope from Ottawa to Vancouver, the prices were: Purolator $10.95; UPS $11.50; FedEx $12.25; Priority Post $12.70.

A recurring theme in submissions to this Review was the complaint that Canada Post's courier services are priced so low and sold so aggressively that other companies - particularly small and medium-sized businesses - find themselves unable to compete.

The experience of one Canadian company, Toronto-based Mowat Express, is illustrative in this regard. The company's president, John Mowat, documented in exceptional detail for the Review, a systematic targeting by Priority Courier and Purolator of Mowat Express' entire business base. The Review is satisfied that the company's account of its experience is credible in its essential elements and that its experience is not unique.

> **THE PRIVATE SECTOR COMPLAINS THAT CANADA POST'S COURIER SERVICES ARE PRICED SO LOW AND SOLD SO AGGRESSIVELY THAT SMALL AND MEDIUM-SIZED BUSINESSES ARE UNABLE TO COMPETE.**

Mowat Express, a family-owned firm established in 1953, describes itself as the largest regional package delivery carrier in Canada, with currently 600 employees and 26 terminals. Its market niche has been providing package delivery and less-than-truckload services primarily to the pharmaceutical/healthcare sector. Since 1994, Canada Post's courier operations have been systematically approaching the company's customers in this sector and offering them, according to Mr. Mowat, rates as much as 20% lower as well as other incentives. The result has been a loss of business so severe that Mowat Express has had to reduce its work force from 700 to 600, and the remaining employees have taken a 10% pay cut.

Mr. Mowat stated at the Review's public meeting that a senior official of Canada Post told his company's vice-president of sales two years ago: "We're going to knock you guys (Mowat Express) off your perch. You're not going to keep this market the way you have." He has subsequently provided to the Review the pertinent details of this encounter in June, 1994.

At the public meeting, Mr. Mowat described Canada Post's sales techniques with his company's customers as follows:

> "You make somebody an offer they can't refuse, a number that the competition can't match and that the customer can't say no to, and

that's gone all the way up to and including blank-sheet presentations to customers: 'Here, we want your business from Mowat. Write down the price you're prepared to pay us to do it, and we'll do business with you.' That is not good old-fashioned competition...In other cases it involves taking the people that make the business decisions (and) entertaining them lavishly - the Skybox, trips to Florida, entertained at the ballet, et cetera."

What is noteworthy about the experience of Mowat Express, in the context of this Review, is that it goes far beyond the simple fact of one company aggressively trying to lure business away from another. This is an entity of the Government of Canada using its market size and position - under the most charitable possible interpretation of the tactics involved - to systematically target the business of a Canadian company to the extent of imperilling its existence.

Other submissions leave no room for hope that this is an isolated instance. To cite just one additional example, Michael Dean - the president of Instant Courier Service, a 17-year-old company with 40 employees - told the Review at its Toronto public meeting:

"Canada Post has been into some of my best customers. They don't go to the corner street lawyer, you know, who wants to argue with his bill every month. They go to the biggest and best customers who they know can pay. They undercut me on some of these mail runs by 50 cents...Even this week a job worth no more than $250...was taken from us and they cut it by $25, the post office...

When there is a massive incursion into the marketplace, like in the case of Priority Post, Purolator, CPC, with full government support and backing, well of course big companies start to lose business and they've been losing thousands, millions, I don't know. But for me the biggest tragedy is that the small ones lose everything and drop out. But you never hear about the small ones dropping out. They just disappear. I think we lose a lot when that happens, as a community..."

It is a finding of the Review that Canada Post is an unfair and inappropriately aggressive competitor in the courier industry.

3.2.3 Appropriateness of Involvement in Courier Industry

A significant number of submissions questioned the appropriateness of Canada Post being involved in the courier industry at all. The point was made that this industry is a mature one with a large number of private sector participants of all sizes. There is no reason for Canada Post to have become so active, it was suggested, in a field that was already well served by private companies.

Interestingly, this view was expressed not only by Canada Post's competitors but also, for example, by the Canadian Industrial Transportation League. The League represents some 400 companies which are large purchasers of transportation, including the services of courier companies. The president of the Canadian Industrial Transportation League, Maria Rehner, told the Review:

> "(The members of the League) have consistently held the view that government ought not to be involved in an area in which the private sector has already established itself...It is our view, therefore, that CPC be asked to divest itself of, at a minimum, the courier enterprise, because the industry does not need a Crown corporation offering service in competition with a litany of private sector operations."

The crux of the League's concern, as explained by Ms Rehner, is that Canada Post will use its privileged position, aggressive pricing and perhaps cross-subsidization to establish market dominance and drive other companies out of the industry. Then it would be in a position to raise prices, and users of courier services would be at a disadvantage in the long run.

The Review will further address the appropriateness of Canada Post's involvement in the courier industry in a later section of this report. Several observations are in order at this point, however.

First, it is difficult to see Canada Post's major sally into the courier industry through the 1993 acquisition of Purolator as anything other than remarkable. The corporation in effect nationalized Canada's largest private sector courier company.

Second, Canada Post's now-massive presence in the courier industry presents a peculiar conflict of interest with regard to its core lettermail responsibilities. The corporation was seeing its lettermail volumes and revenues eroded by courier companies which offered faster and more reliable delivery. It responded not by improving the speed of its lettermail service, but by becoming increasingly involved in the courier business, culminating in the Purolator purchase.

As the corporation's own Coopers & Lybrand report comments, its standards of service for mail "are less ambitious than most other postal administrations."[18] But if its courier operations are indeed as profitable as Canada Post claims, what possible incentive could it now have to improve lettermail service? If it can charge $8.45 to deliver a letter from Ottawa to Toronto the next

> **CANADA POST IN EFFECT NATIONALIZED CANADA'S LARGEST PRIVATE SECTOR COURIER COMPANY.**

day by Priority Post, or $9.95 by Purolator, why would it want to deliver that letter the next day for 45 cents? If anything, sound business strategy under these circumstances might suggest making lettermail service sufficiently poor to convert as many users as possible to its courier services. That, surely, is not the intended mandate of the corporation.

3.3 Competition with Mailing Centres

Mailing centres are a relatively new type of business that began to develop in Canada in the 1980s. They are, in essence, one-stop business centres which act as agents for their customers by providing them with parcel packing and shipping services, along with a wide range of other business-related needs. They advise customers on which carrier or courier company can best transport the particular envelope or parcel according to specified needs, and they then make the necessary arrangements. Business-related services offered by these centres often include faxing, photocopying, production of business cards and rubber stamps, word-processing, mailbox rental, mail preparation, telephone answering, electronic money transfers, report binding and even gift-wrapping and key-cutting.

There are an estimated 300 to 400 such mailing centres across Canada, employing approximately 2,000 people. Some of these centres are part of

---

[18]Coopers & Lybrand Consulting, *Choices for a Self-Sustaining Canada Post*, op. cit.; page 26.

franchise chains such as Mail Boxes Etc. and Pak Mail; others are independently owned.

It appears, based on submissions made to the Review, that Canada Post has effectively declared war on this business sector, after having initially worked cooperatively with it. Hillaine Kroft, owner of Pack & Post in Winnipeg, told the Review that when she started her business in 1989,

> "...Canada Post, through its Commercial Customer Representative was a ready, willing and able, not to mention cooperative and helpful, ally, and could not have been more encouraging. The representative came by often to instruct us on how to properly register mail, fill out waybills, to deliver supplies, and just generally check on how we were getting along. We were considered a commercial account, and as such had a contract for daily pick-up, account privileges with Priority Post, and enjoyed a mutually beneficial relationship. We bought our stamps at a Canada Post franchise...Canada Post carried by far the majority of our parcels and priority mail...We utilized the services of other carriers as circumstances warranted, but no one seemed to have a problem with that."

This relationship changed in 1993, as Ms Kroft told the Review:

> "In the summer of that year, the Corporation threatened cancellation of all contracts with our company and ordered us to cease any and all use of its products and services in conducting our business. They even called our postage meter supplier and challenged their right to rent us a meter...On more than one of the many harassing visits paid by Canada Post's representatives, I was told that the reason I could no longer use Canada Post's products and services in my business was because I also offered alternative courier services. When I asked on one occasion whether they would reconsider if I would guarantee Canada Post a certain percentage of our parcel business, the response was, ' Make me an offer '."

Robert Marshall, owner of a Pak Mail franchise in Markham, Ont., gave the Review a virtually identical account:

> "In early 1993 we were advised that our contracts would not be honoured any longer. There was little explanation as to why, other than the fact that we were considered in competition with the post office and their own postal franchisees...The statement was made that if we gave up dealing with the competitors of Canada Post, there would certainly be no problem in us continuing to use the services of Canada Post."

This behaviour, as described to the Review in these two submissions and several others, sounds remarkably like "exclusive dealing", which is covered under the Civil Provisions of the Competition Act.

Canada Post offers quite different rationales for its dealings with mailing centres. It argues that these centres fail to meet its requirements for contracts permitting them to sell stamps and provide other Canada Post services, because they refuse to sell Canada Post services exclusively. The corporation also argues that it is protecting its own franchisees from encroachment by the centres, and even that it is protecting consumers from mistaking the mailing centres for Canada Post outlets.

The mailing centres respond that they are not retailers of stamps, but rather their end users in providing a broader service to clients. They cite the analogy of lawyers, for instance, who write letters on their clients' behalf, send them through the mail and then charge the clients for the postage as part of their fees. The centres also deny that they compete directly with Canada Post franchisees, pointing out that many of these franchisees are drug stores or supermarkets which sell only a very limited selection of packing supplies and which do not offer the same range of business-related services.

The Review finds these arguments persuasive. It also notes that both Canada Post and Purolator have opened their own business centres offering services patterned on the mailing service companies and competing with them. It is difficult, consequently, to confidently attribute Canada Post's actions to anything other than aggressive competitiveness.

> IT IS A VERY SERIOUS MATTER INDEED FOR A PUBLIC SECTOR MONOPOLY TO WITHHOLD FROM SMALL BUSINESSES ITS MONOPOLY SERVICES WHICH ARE VITAL OR NEARLY VITAL TO THEIR EXISTENCE.

In any event, Canada Post's response to the mailing centres, including the refusal to make pick-ups or deliveries, seems disproportionate to any possible challenge posed by them. It is a very serious matter indeed for a public sector monopoly to withhold from small businesses its monopoly services which are vital or nearly vital to their existence. Canada Post Corporation might have been expected to understand that a corollary of the exclusive privilege should be an obligation, except in the most dramatic of circumstances, not to deny any individual or business in Canada the services that are routinely available to everyone else.

It is a finding of the Review that Canada Post is an unfair competitor in its dealings with mailing services.

3.4 The Issue of Cross-subsidization

Allegations that Canada Post uses its revenues from the lettermail monopoly to cross-subsidize its commercial competitive businesses have been a recurring theme almost since the day the Crown corporation was created.

The Review has made every effort to explore this issue in depth, including extensive analysis by a seconded Review staff member who is a senior investigator with the Competition Bureau. Nevertheless, there is no expectation that its findings will fully satisfy everyone, particularly since the corporation's insistence on "commercial secrecy" precludes making public the detailed figures on which they are based. It is also necessary to note that the Review did not conduct an audit of Canada Post. Analysis was based on the data it was possible to obtain from the corporation, and is therefore limited to some extent by the limitations of Canada Post's own accounting methodologies. Despite this, a clear enough picture has emerged, in the opinion of the Review, to provide a suitable basis for policy recommendations.

It is important, at the outset, to dispose of one ongoing source of confusion. Canada Post has consistently maintained that, in reviewing its acquisition of Purolator in 1993, the Competition Bureau exonerated the corporation of all allegations of cross-subsidization. In its submission to this Review, Canada Post states:

> "The Bureau's *'Backgrounder'*, released at the time approval was granted, states in part: '...the Director was satisfied that Canada Post has not engaged in the practice of cross-subsidization and that grounds do not exist to believe that such behaviour is likely to occur in the future'."[19]

When they appeared at the Review's public meeting on behalf of the Director of Investigation and Research, senior officials of the Competition Bureau were read this passage from the Canada Post submission and invited to comment. They responded that the examination to which Canada Post alludes was confined to specific technical questions pertaining only to

---

[19]Canada Post Corporation, *Ensuring Universal Services at Affordable Rates,* op.cit.; page 22.

merger analysis of the Purolator acquisition. Robert Lancop, chief of the Bureau's Civil Matters Branch, went on to say:

> "I think there has been a great deal of press and a lot of claims by Canada Post to the effect that we have given them a clean bill of health, and that is really not the case."

As well, Gilles Menard, the Bureau's Deputy Director of Investigation and Research, Civil Matters Branch, referred to the "allegations that have been made before this Committee (the Review) of all sorts of practices engaged in by Canada Post that are said to be anti-competitive." He further said:

> "The Director has also received a number of these complaints, or similar complaints, which range from allegations of abuse of monopoly on the part of Canada Post, tied selling, refusal to deal, market restrictions, including product repricing. The Director takes all these allegations very, very seriously."

None of this means that the corporation necessarily *is* cross-subsidizing, of course. But the mantle of vindication by the Competition Bureau is not currently available to Canada Post.

There are two basic categories of cross-subsidization: direct/explicit, and indirect/implicit. As well, leveraging is technically subject to consideration within the category of direct/implicit subsidization, but will here be addressed separately. Each of these three issue areas will be examined in turn. Since this is a very technically complex field, the Review will confine itself to briefly summarizing the principal findings, without venturing into a level of detail inappropriate in a report of this nature.

> **THE MANTLE OF VINDICATION BY THE COMPETITION BUREAU IS NOT CURRENTLY AVAILABLE TO CANADA POST.**

3.4.1 Direct/Explicit Cross-subsidization

Direct/explicit cross-subsidization usually entails the transfer of revenues directly from one product line to finance the costs of another. This assumes that all costs are correctly identified and assigned appropriately to each product.

The allegations of direct cross-subsidization by Canada Post relate to cross-funding of competitive products by lettermail and other exclusive products, and the leveraging of the network. (Leveraging will be addressed separately). In alleging that the corporation is using lettermail to fund other products, competitors have most often cited as evidence the fact that 74% of Canada Post's contribution is generated by lettermail, even though it represents only 45% of volumes.

The Review finds first, that this interpretation of the figures is based on a misapprehension. Lettermail's apparently low share of volume is due to the role played by admail in increasing total volume without making a particularly large contribution. This is because admail, a very low-priced product which does not incur the expensive forwarding, processing or sorting costs of other mail, is generally discounted for very large volumes. If admail is removed from the total equation, then the percentages for lettermail change to 76% contribution and 71% of volume. The allegation may therefore be characterized as comparing apples and oranges: since the products have such different costing and pricing patterns, it is not technically sound to automatically infer cross-subsidization.

Second, even if the figures were correctly interpreted, the approach is conceptually flawed. The difficulty arises from the fact that Canada Post has certain common costs which are impossible to attribute to any specific product or product line in a way that everyone will agree is "accurate". The following example is illustrative:

♦ A company has two products, lettermail and admail. Both products use a delivery network which operates every day regardless of whether only lettermail, only admail, or both types of mail are being delivered. The company has the following costs in millions of dollars:

	$
costs to run the network	100.
costs to deliver lettermail	50.
costs to deliver admail	10.
total costs	160.

♦ The company has the following revenues in millions of dollars:

	$
revenues from lettermail	115
revenues from admail	50
total revenues	165

♦ The company's net income is therefore $5 million. If this company delivered only lettermail, it would have a loss of $35 million (revenues of $115 million minus total costs of $150 million). If it delivered only admail, it would lose $60 million (revenues of $50 million minus total costs of $110 million). While the company is clearly more profitable delivering both products than only delivering either one, this raises the question of how the network costs should be apportioned. If, for instance, each product is to pay its costs plus a "fair" share of the network costs, fair could be defined in various ways. If it is assumed to mean an equal share, the results would be:

lettermail

	$	$	$
total costs	50. +	50. =	100.
total revenues	115.		
net income	15.		

admail

	$	$	$
total costs	50. +	10. =	60.
total revenues	50.		
net income	-10.		

Thus, theoretically, lettermail is "cross-subsidizing" admail by $10 million. But if a fair share of costs was defined instead to mean an equal share of *total* costs, and each product's share was therefore $80 million, lettermail would be cross-subsidizing admail not by $10 million but by $30 million. And if costs were apportioned, say, relative to each product's share of total revenues, admail would be making a *positive* contribution.

This approach to cross-subsidization was applied to the financial cost data of Canada Post taken from the 1995 Annual Cost Study. The results vary with how costs are assigned to each particular product. Depending on the particular product being considered, a case can often be made that lettermail is or is not financing the costs of that product. There is no "correct" answer to allocating the total costs in a fair way. Consequently, allegations that Canada Post is directly cross-funding its competitive products with revenues from the exclusive privilege can neither be definitively substantiated nor disproved. Everything depends on the assumptions used.

3.4.2 Indirect/Implicit Cross-subsidization

Implicit cross-subsidization refers to the incorrect assigning of costs across product lines. If cross-subsidization of any significance is taking place within Canada Post, it is in the form of implicit cross-subsidization in which costs related to competitive products are misallocated and shifted onto the exclusive privilege line of products.

In 1987, Canada Post introduced an Activity Based Costing system (ABC) to use as the basis for its Annual Cost Study. The purpose of this system is essentially to distinguish between common network costs which remain unallocated, and the incremental costs of providing any given product or group of products. The ABC system assigns all types of costs (fixed and variable) to products that are associated with an activity performed in their production.

But despite the use of the ABC system, there is still an incentive for a company like Canada Post to underestimate the magnitude of the incremental costs and overstate the magnitude of the common, non-allocated costs. The use of the ABC system has simply translated the initial incentive into disincentive to rigorously apply the cost system to its maximum potential. As sophisticated as the corporation's ABC system is, there is still considerable latitude to exercise discretion in deciding what should or should not be included in the definition of incremental costs.

An examination of Canada Post's non-allocated cost categories has revealed that this discretion in its methodology has led to a number of incidents of cost misallocation. The failure in the methodology to correctly allocate costs was generally found to be related to either how the concept of time was treated in determining long-run incremental costs, or to how the causal links between products and activities were identified or ignored.

There is no evidence that Canada Post deliberately sets out to misallocate costs to its own advantage, but its level of diligence appears to be affected by the fact that there is virtually no penalty if such favourable misallocation occurs. If the volume variability component of an activity is obvious and easily measured, then the costs of that

> **ALLOCATION BECOMES THE EXCEPTION RATHER THAN THE RULE, BECAUSE THERE IS NO REAL PENALTY TO CANADA POST FOR GETTING IT WRONG.**

activity will be allocated. Where it is not obvious and/or difficult to measure, allocation is unlikely to occur. Allocation becomes the exception rather than the rule, because there is no real penalty to Canada Post for getting it wrong.

Without entering into excessive technical detail, it suffices to say here that the work of the Review identified a total of $180 million in unallocated costs that Canada Post has agreed could have been allocated and will be allocated in future. This will reduce the non-allocated portion of the corporation's total costs from 44% to 41%. The Review notes that allocation of these previously non-allocated costs has a dramatic effect on the contribution levels of three product groups: parcels, courier, and "other". As well, the work of the Review identified another $60 million which could be allocatable, but which would require detailed costing and engineering studies.

To the extent that cost misallocation is a form of cross-subsidization, it is a finding of this Review that Canada Post has cross-subsidized. Specific product lines were relieved from being directly responsible for paying a portion of their costs. When the misallocated costs that could be measured were reallocated, the contribution margins on certain products - parcels and courier, for example - declined in value. But their contributions still remain positive. Thus Canada Post is able to argue that cross-subsidization does not occur.

Nevertheless, Canada Post has misallocated its costs. Deliberate or not, this has given its competitive products an advantage over those of Canada Post's competitors that they would otherwise not have. Whether this actually places competitors at a significant disadvantage, is to some degree irrelevant if fairness is the only factor being considered. To the extent that Canada Post's ability to misallocate its costs flows directly from being a Crown corporation endowed with a Government-granted monopoly, this can be characterized as an unfair use of its privileged position.

> **TO THE EXTENT THAT COST MISALLOCATION IS A FORM OF CROSS-SUBSIDIZATION, IT IS A FINDING OF THIS REVIEW THAT CANADA POST HAS CROSS-SUBSIDIZED.**

3.4.3 Leveraging

Canada Post's competitors complain that the corporation is able to use its network to leverage cost savings for its competitive products. They point to such activities as piggybacking lettermail onto Purolator flights, piggybacking courier products onto mail trucks, and combining services in the provision of volume electronic mail, media cards and the operation of business centres.

Canada Post openly admits that it does and will continue to leverage its existing network to achieve cost savings in the provision of all its product lines. It argues that this is merely efficient use of resources and sound business practice.

The difficulty is that, for instance, by using the same airline as Purolator for its lettermail shipments, Canada Post is causing the overall costs per piece of transporting both products to decline through volume discounts. The fact that the planes continue to be used primarily for Purolator packages, with Canada Post making up the remaining capacity, indicates that both volumes are necessary to obtain the lower costs per unit. Since Purolator could not have procured such discounts in any other manner, Purolator's costs are lower than they would otherwise be - as a direct result of Canada Post's exclusive privilege. To the extent that Purolator's competitors do not have access to the same volumes and resulting discounts, this constitutes unfair advantage.

The same sort of argument applies to using Canada Post's mail trucks to carry a variety of competitive products including courier, Xpresspost, and admail. In the case of Volume Electronic Mail, likewise, the corporation appears to be cross-subsidizing its production services with its delivery service.

The leveraging issue underscores the fundamental problem with Canada Post's competitive activity. It is undoubtedly true that other multi-product companies regularly use leveraging of their networks to maximize efficiency - but these private sector companies did not build their networks with public funds, on the foundation of a government-granted monopoly.

> **PRIVATE SECTOR COMPANIES THAT LEVERAGE THEIR NETWORKS DID NOT BUILD THEIR NETWORKS ON PUBLIC FUNDS.**

None of Canada Post's competitors have access to the cost advantages that leveraging such a network automatically provides.

In the opinion of the Review, consequently, the position of the corporation is not made acceptable by a simple finding that its competitive product lines are not actually losing money. Because any contribution they make is really "gravy" - additional revenues to offset network costs that would be incurred in any event - it does not necessarily matter to the corporation if these contributions are relatively small. This enables Canada Post to charge prices lower than would make sense for its competitors. The conclusion is inescapable that this makes Canada Post an unfair competitor.

3.5 Summary of Competitive Stance

On the basis of the above considerations, the Review has reached the following conclusions about the competitive stance of Canada Post:

FINDING # 2: In its competitive activities with regard to unaddressed admail, courier services, and mailing centres, Canada Post Corporation is an unfair competitor in ways detrimental to private sector companies. Further, the corporation's misallocation of costs constitutes a form of cross-subsidization, whether intentional or otherwise. And its ability to leverage a network built up with public funds on the strength of a government-granted monopoly gives it a pricing advantage over competitors that is seriously unfair.

4 The Corporate Culture of Canada Post Corporation

4.1 From Public to Private Orientation

The post office has a long history of public service to Canada and to Canadians. It is hardly possible to overstate the role it has played in opening up the Canadian nation and in promoting the country's economic and social development. If ever there was an organization deeply rooted in a commitment to nation-building, in the values of the public service and in reaching out to serve all Canadians, it was the post office.

The ethos underlying our postal service was cogently summarized in Parliament before the turn of the century:

> "Post Offices are not established for the purpose of providing a revenue, but for the convenience of the people. They have been established on the same principle as that which has guided us in undertaking public works, not with the hope of obtaining a revenue but in the view that the general business of the community will be promoted by them."[20]

All this clearly began to change when the post office was turned into a Crown corporation in 1981. Its long-established public service values and goals were cast into head-to-head competition with new, purely commercial goals.

This occurred because the creators of Canada Post Corporation sought to achieve two outcomes at once: to transform the Post Office Department into a Crown corporation pursuing commercial objectives leading to financial self-sufficiency, and to continue promoting longstanding public policy objectives such as universality of service. No attempt was made to separate commercial operations from public policy objectives, nor even to specify a relative hierarchy of importance. The inevitable tensions between a public

---

[20]House of Commons, *Debates*, 4 February 1884.

policy orientation and a commercial one were simply internalized in the Canada Post mandate.

With regard to the public policy objectives, the Canada Post Corporation Act does commit Canada Post to "maintaining basic customary postal service" and to "providing a standard of service that will meet the needs of the people of Canada and that is similar with respect to communities of the same size." But these rather unspecific commitments are on the same footing as the requirement to "conduct its operations on a self-sustaining financial basis". Also on the same footing is the authorization to provide services and products "incidental" to the postal services as well as "services that, in the opinion of the Corporation, are capable of being conveniently provided in the course of carrying out the other objects of the Corporation."

This contrasts significantly with, for instance, the United States postal legislation which states in its first paragraph:

> "...the Postal Service shall have as its basic function the obligation to provide postal services to bind the Nation together through the personal, educational, literary and business correspondence of the people. It shall provide prompt, reliable and efficient services to patrons in all areas and shall render postal services to all communities. The costs of establishing and maintaining the Postal Service shall not be apportioned to impair the overall value of such services to the people."[21]

The second paragraph goes on to add:

> "The Postal Service shall provide a maximum degree of effective and regular postal services to rural areas, communities, and small towns where post offices are not self-sustaining. No small post office shall be closed solely for operating at a deficit, it being the specific intent of the Congress that effective postal services be ensured to residents of both urban and rural communities."[22]

---

[21]United States Government Manual, *United States Postal Service*, part 1, chapter 2, section 101; 1995; page 7.

[22]Ibid.

In the case of Canada Post, a number of public policy functions are carried out with specific financial compensation from the Government. Processing Parliamentary mail free of postage is the only such function explicitly imposed by statute, and the Government transfers $11 million a year to the corporation for this service.

As well, the Government has since 1986-87 been paying Canada Post an annual fee of $3 million a year to handle materials for the use of the blind free of charge. It is envisioned that the Canadian Heritage Department will transfer approximately $53 million a year to the corporation to provide reduced postage rates for eligible publications under the new Publications Assistance Program which replaces the former postal subsidy. And, finally, the Department of Indian Affairs and Northern Development compensates Canada Post for the Northern Air Stage Commercial Freight Service under which perishable foods and other goods are delivered to remote communities at the reduced rate; payment to the corporation is estimated at $15.6 million.

> THE CORE PUBLIC POLICY RESPONSIBILITIES OF CANADA POST ARE TWO-FOLD: TO PROVIDE ALL CANADIANS WITH UNIVERSAL MAIL SERVICE AT A UNIFORM, AFFORDABLE PRICE, AND TO SERVE AS A NATION-WIDE PRESENCE OF THE FEDERAL GOVERNMENT.

These services, whose combined cost of $82.6 million a year is relatively small in the context of Canada Post's total operations, are important but not fundamental to the corporation's public policy role. They could all be provided in alternative ways in the absence of a public sector postal service.

The core public policy responsibilities of Canada Post - the responsibilities which are the reason for its existence as an entity of the national government - are two-fold: to provide all Canadians with universal mail service at a uniform, affordable price, and to serve as a nation-wide presence of the Federal Government. Because Canada Post is present in virtually every community across the country, this corporation - probably more than any other institution - is the day-to-day face of the Government of Canada. Consequently, it has an opportunity and a *responsibility*, in the opinion of the Review, to maximize the value of this presence by serving all Canadians in a manner that promotes national unity and makes the strongest possible contribution to quality of life.

These core responsibilities have not been receiving the priority they deserve, particularly since 1986. In that year, the undefined and uneasy balance between the public policy responsibilities and commercial objectives of Canada Post was tipped when the Government of the day ordered the corporation to give absolute and urgent priority to financially breaking even, whatever the consequence to its public policy goals. Within Canada Post, commercial orientation became the overriding focus.

The then President of Canada Post, Donald Lander, stated in late 1986:

> "The operation of Canada Post Corporation...is bringing about a form of...privatization, albeit the owner is still the Canadian government and its people. But with the methodologies in which we are now approaching Canada Post, trying to bring in the values that are inherent in other corporations, I believe that is a form of privatization in its relationship to its responsibilities, its measurement of its assets, and its return on those investments that heretofore under a department was not possible...the corporation...is evolving into a private, corporate-value entity...the cultural change is to a private corporation."[23]

4.2 Impact on Corporate Culture

This internal "privatization" of Canada Post appears to be at the root of many of the corporation's current difficulties. Public enterprises exist to serve a public purpose and to provide a public good; private enterprises exist to make money for their owners or shareholders and to meet a commercial demand.

These fundamental differences of purpose are inevitably translated into differences of approach. A public good is, by definition, non-discriminatory, in the sense that everyone who comes forward for a given service or product should be treated the same. Private interests, on the other hand, have a right to concentrate their efforts on the customers who are most lucrative or easiest to handle. This explains, for instance, why private schools or hospitals often appear more successful than their public-sector counterparts,

---

[23]Standing Committee on Government Operations, *Minutes of Proceedings and Evidence*, 4 December 1986, no.6, page 37.

because the former are able to screen out the most difficult, the most costly or the least promising students or patients.

When a public enterprise like Canada Post almost wholly adopts the values and priorities of the private sector, as has become the case, problems are virtually inevitable. Once the bottom-line stands alone as the dominant consideration, the temptation becomes irresistible to favour lucrative business customers over individual citizens, large corporations over small businesses, or densely-populated urban centres over rural areas.

Such behaviors, indeed, are at the crux of many of the complaints that were brought to the attention of the Review. Unaddressed admail is sometimes given priority treatment over community newspapers, for instance, not because advertising flyers are a greater social good than newspapers, but because Canada Post sees them as a good source of revenue. Closings of rural post offices and the lack of delivery standards in rural areas are motivated not by a drive to serve Canadians better, but by a desire to minimize costs.

> **THE UNFAIR COMPETITIVE ACTIVITIES ARE A DIRECT CONSEQUENCE OF CANADA POST'S ATTEMPT TO FUNCTION LIKE A COMMERCIALLY-ORIENTED PRIVATE COMPANY DESPITE ITS PRIVILEGED STATUS AS AN UNREGULATED PUBLIC SECTOR MONOPOLY.**

The unfair competitive activities explored in the previous section are a direct consequence of Canada Post's attempt to function like a commercially-oriented private company despite its privileged status as an unregulated public sector monopoly. Under such circumstances, the appearance and indeed the reality of unfairness are virtually unavoidable.

Beyond the aggressive nature of the competitive activities themselves, however, the Review has also found cause for serious concern that the emphasis on commercial objectives has distorted the corporate culture of Canada Post.

The internal culture of a public sector organization is appropriately focused on serving the public interest. The culture of a private sector business is normally focused on competing as strongly as possible to maximize profits. The internal "privatization" of Canada Post appears to have led to a culture based on the belief that the corporation serves the public interest *by* competing as aggressively as possible in pursuit of commercial profits - and that it is therefore entitled to use its powerful position as an entity of the Government to overcome obstacles to this activity.

At the public meeting in Vancouver, Jon Hoff, appearing on behalf of the Independent Mailing Service Providers association, told the Review:

> "When we take our product to Canada Post, we must submit a Statement of Mailing that includes the client name and other confidential client information. The regulations say so and, fair enough, we comply. What does Canada Post do with this information that is entrusted to it in its capacity as the steward of the exclusive privilege? It takes this confidential information supplied by our industry and markets against us directly to our own clients. By any standards, this is a breach of confidence..."

At the public meeting in Toronto, Normand Moreau, President of Campbell Abbot Laser Mail referred to this allegation by the Independent Mailing Service Providers, and stated:

> "We wish to confirm our group's experience with similar unethical business practices. The direct customer solicitation by Canada Post occurs too frequently for us to accept the official response that it is not Canada Post policy to bypass the mailing service provider and solicit clients directly."

The Review was presented with other similar allegations, including allegations from community newspapers that Canada Post uses confidential information supplied by them to solicit their advertising clients. The Review has received documentary materials in support of allegations of unfair use of confidential information by Canada Post.

In Winnipeg, Hillaine Kroft, owner of a small business centre called Pack & Post, told the Review at its public meeting:

> "It is wrong to stand outside a store and interrogate and search people performing pick-up services. It is wrong to seize goods brought to the post office by private courier unless there is a legal or safety reason. It is wrong to come into a store and threaten and harass and bully staff in the name of performing an essential monopoly service. Canada Post management...has conducted itself in just such an immoral and illegal way."

The Montreal newspaper La Presse reported in April that Canada Post sales representatives in Longueuil had induced Canada Post letter carriers to photocopy envelopes sent by courier companies to their clients. The purpose was to identify the clients of various courier companies, so that Canada Post sales representatives could approach these clients and try to win them away.

While Canada Post has characterized these various alleged improprieties as isolated incidents, there comes a point where an accumulation of seemingly isolated incidents becomes a pattern. The Review is concerned that the matters cited here, and others that were brought to its attention, constitute such a pattern.

The Review was not endowed with the investigative powers or resources to independently establish the accuracy of each individual allegation. Nevertheless, when a significant number of Canadians of apparent good faith have reason to believe that an entity of the Government of Canada is engaged in such practices, that in itself is a serious problem. When written materials lend substance to at least some of those beliefs, the problem is intensified.

To its credit, the corporation has stated that such practices are not condoned. Regrettably, however, it chose to respond by engaging the consulting firm of KPMG to investigate by contacting the individuals and organizations who made allegations to the Review. Some of those contacted have, not altogether surprisingly, complained that they perceive this as intimidation.

The President of Canada Post, Mr. Clermont, was asked at the Toronto public meeting about the various allegations of improper behavior on the part of the corporation. Aspects of his response did not dispel the Review's concerns about the current corporate culture at Canada Post:

> "When an organization has been a monopoly for a hundred and some years and when there were really very few alternatives, it is only natural that once it enters the competitive world it is driven by personal initiatives, and we encourage it. It is driven by a wish to win, which we can only commend...These incidents do occur. They will occur...As soon as we

hear something like this, steps are taken to correct the situation...We can't stifle people's initiatives."

The concept of a powerful public sector monopoly pitted in competition against small private companies and "driven by a wish to win," is not reassuring. In fact, the Review was presented with disturbing evidence that some Canadians are so convinced of Canada Post's wish to win that they are afraid of the corporation.

For instance, Gary Winsor, the president of Budget Flyer Delivery, drove five hours from New Brunswick in a snowstorm to tell the Review at its Halifax public meeting about what he perceived as unfair competition by Canada Post. But he expressed reluctance to suggest changes, for fear of retaliation by the corporation:

> "I am just a little worried about what kind of repercussions I am going to get when I get back to Bathurst, as I am delivering mail to Canada Post. I am a customer, and it has been shaky in the last number of years because I have been a customer and at the same being a competitor, and it's touch-and-go in that respect."

In Toronto, J. Michael Dean, president of Instant Courier Service, told the Review that many other small couriers were reluctant to complain publicly about Canada Post because they are "scared of any reprisals they may have against them." He explained:

> "They feel that if they speak out against their post office or against the government, that maybe they may suffer in some way by it."

Gerry Dorge, appearing on behalf of the Canadian Community Newspapers Association at the Ottawa public meeting of the Review, said:

> "I can tell you that three members that we know of chose not to appear before this Review because of their fear of Canada Post seeking reprisals...I can tell you of a couple of experiences I personally have gone through over the last couple of weeks since I first appeared in front of you in Winnipeg. I got a call from Canada Post on an issue - I hadn't heard from Canada Post in six years - on a niggly issue...Are those things coincidental? Quite possibly, but it does raise our suspicions...So we do know that there are some publishers very fearful of offending, if you will, Canada Post."

Subsequent to the public meetings, the Canadian Community Newspapers Association brought to the attention of the Review several instances of behaviors by Canada Post that its members understandably perceive as retaliation for having made submissions to the Review. Again, the Review was not in a position to conduct detailed investigations. But the very fact that apparently reasonable Canadians dealing with an entity of the Government of Canada are experiencing fear, and perceiving retaliation, is itself a serious concern.

It is unacceptable that any citizens of the Canadian democracy should have cause to fear their own government or any of its entities. There are Canadians afraid of Canada Post, not unreasonably in the opinion of the Review, and this is an indication that the emphasis of recent years on commercialization and competition has gravely distorted Canada Post's corporate culture.

On the basis of the above considerations, the Review has reached the following conclusions about the state of the corporate culture at Canada Post:

FINDING # 3: **The shift to a predominantly commercial orientation in the years since 1986 has deflected Canada Post from its core public policy responsibilities and gravely distorted its corporate culture. This has produced serious and credible allegations of improper behaviors, as well as a situation in which a significant number of Canadians feel afraid of an entity of their own government.**

---

5 The Strategic Focus of Canada Post Corporation

Canada Post's strategic emphasis on competing with the private sector in areas outside its core public policy responsibilities is founded on two key premises. First, the corporation believes it must have revenues from competitive activities to help finance its core postal responsibilities. Second, Canada Post believes that it must diversify increasingly into competitive fields to insulate itself from the financial consequences of anticipated declines in lettermail volumes.

5.1 Supplementing Revenues

In its submission to the Review, the corporation states the first premise as follows:

> "The scale and scope of the distribution network required for universal letter services in turn requires that CPC also provide competitive services that generate contributions in excess of their incremental costs and thus defray overhead and other fixed costs of the network."[24]

The first point to be made about this strategic approach is that, empirically, it has not worked very well. As detailed in preceding sections, the years of emphasis on competitive activities have not yet produced sufficient revenues even to allow the corporation to consistently achieve break-even status. From a strategic point of view, it is not necessarily true that if something has been unsuccessful in the past, continuing to do it in the future will produce better results.

Second, the emphasis on competitive activities has created serious problems for Canada Post and, through it, for the Government. Attempting to compete aggressively from its position as an unregulated public sector

---

[24]Canada Post Corporation, *Ensuring Universal Service at Affordable Rates*, op.cit.; page 34.

monopoly has made the corporation an unfair competitor, distorted its corporate culture and led to serious concerns about the corporation's behavior.

The third, and perhaps most fundamental, shortcoming of this approach is that it has distracted Canada Post from the core public policy responsibilities that are the reason for its existence. The corporation exists, ultimately, to deliver the mail, and yet its most visible preoccupations in recent years have been with the establishment and expansion of various competitive activities.

A noteworthy aspect of this distraction is that it has led Canada Post to invest both money and attention in ventures of highly questionable merit. In 1992, for instance, the corporation acquired a 12% share in GD Net, an international courier and delivery operation, for $32.4 million. It subsequently sank another $5.3 million into the venture. In June of this year, Canada Post sold its share at a net loss of $5.1 million.

> THE CORPORATION EXISTS, ULTIMATELY, TO DELIVER THE MAIL, AND YET ITS MOST VISIBLE PREOCCUPATIONS IN RECENT YEARS HAVE BEEN WITH THE ESTABLISHMENT AND EXPANSION OF VARIOUS COMPETITIVE ACTIVITIES.

Similarly, Canada Post has invested to be a participant in the UBI initiative, a pilot project for interactive TV service in Quebec. The corporation's Phase I investment is only set at $17 million, but staying involved through Phase II would cost a total in excess of $34 million. The project is currently two years behind schedule, is in a field where Canada Post has no expertise or credentials, and is likely to be overtaken by a technology explosion led by competitors including IBM, Microsoft, Apple and hundreds of other corporations. Aside from the money involved, engaging in such activities in the name of maximizing its competitive presence is a significant digression from what should be Canada Post's core strategic focus: the lettermail service which is the reason for its existence.

5.2 Anticipating Volume Declines

In its submission to the Review, Canada Post summarizes the second premise behind its emphasis on competitive activities as follows:

> "As lettermail business is lost to courier, electronic and other alternatives, CPC can best protect itself by supplying competitive services that meet market needs."[25]

The assumption that Canada Post needs major diversification to protect itself against lettermail volume declines is open to question on several counts. It is by no means clear that lettermail volumes will decline dramatically in the short to medium-term future. And if lettermail volumes were indeed to collapse, it is even less clear that sidestepping into other fields in competition with the private sector is an appropriate public policy response for Canada Post.

Lettermail volumes are currently flat or growing slightly, not in decline. Opinions differ as to the long-term prospects, but experts consulted by the Review generally agree that there is not likely to be a dramatic fall in North American lettermail volumes for at least five years, perhaps ten. The composition of the volumes may change - for instance, there may be fewer consumer billings, but more targeted direct mail. But paper-based communication sent by mail is, according to the experts, widely considered likely to remain with us for some time to come.

With regard to the specific alternatives cited by Canada Post, there is no obvious reason why large further volumes of lettermail need be lost to couriers *if* the corporation provides sufficiently speedy and reliable mail delivery service. As for electronic alternatives, the penetration into households is still sufficiently low that there is no evidence to suggest the likelihood of a major impact on lettermail volumes over the next five years. The more probable scenario appears to be that lettermail and other emerging forms of communication can co-exist for quite some time, sharing a growing total market for all forms of communication.

---

[25]Canada Post Corporation, *Ensuring Universal Service at Affordable Rates*, op.cit.; page 35.

Were lettermail volumes to begin declining dramatically at some point, it is questionable in any event whether Canada Post's diversification strategy would be sensible or appropriate. Such a strategy would mean that the more its lettermail volumes and revenues declined, the further Canada Post would have to reach into the private sector to compete for revenues from other sorts of activities.

Less and less of the corporation's business would be the core postal services that are its public policy reason for existing. And as its revenues from the core services declined, Canada Post would be in the situation of an addict needing an ever stronger fix: it would have to compete more and more aggressively, in more and more private sector areas, to compensate for progressively larger lettermail revenue shortfalls.

Lettermail either is a sunset industry, or it is not. If it is not, then there is little rationale for Canada Post to focus on diversifying instead of concentrating on achieving excellence in its core postal business. And if it is a sunset industry, there is no obvious public policy rationale for Canada Post to invent a new commercially-oriented role for itself instead of being gradually phased out and having its outlets converted into a different form of federal presence if, as and when a post office is no longer needed.

The above considerations lead the Review to the following conclusion:

> **FINDING # 4: Canada Post Corporation's strategic vision of expanding into competitive activities to supplement revenues and to protect itself against anticipated lettermail volume declines is imperfect in practice and in principle. In practice, the years of emphasis on competition have produced more distractions and problems than financial successes. In principle, Canada Post should concentrate on excellence in its core lettermail responsibilities as long as they are relevant, and be treated as a sunset industry and phased out if the time ever comes when they are no longer relevant.**

6 The Governance of Canada Post Corporation

Canada Post is subject, in theory, to supervision and control by five principal authorities: the Minister Responsible for Canada Post, the Treasury Board, the Minister of Finance, the Crown Corporations Directorate, and the corporation's own Board of Directors. In addition, the Cabinet and Parliament play an infrequent and less direct role.

The Minister's formal supervisory responsibilities include appointing or recommending to the Governor-in-Council, (the Cabinet), the appointment of Canada Post's directors; recommending to the Governor-in-Council the approval of its corporate plans, budgets, borrowing and payments of surpluses; tabling in Parliament its annual reports and summaries of corporate plans and budgets; recommending that the Governor-in-Council issue directives to Canada Post when necessary, and tabling such directives in Parliament.

The Treasury Board is responsible for reviewing the strategic direction of Canada Post's corporate plan; reviewing proposed decisions or recommendations of a financial nature made by the Minister Responsible for Canada Post; and approving the corporation's capital budget and certain transactions. The Minister of Finance has authority over actions by Canada Post that could affect the Government's fiscal framework, including the corporation's borrowing and the payment of any surpluses.

The Crown Corporations Directorate, a joint organization of the Treasury Board Secretariat and the Department of Finance, is responsible for the control and accountability framework prescribed for Canada Post as a Crown corporation. It monitors the corporation's activities, resources, plans and performance.

The corporation's Board of Directors has four broad areas of responsibility: establishing the corporation's strategic direction, safeguarding the corporation's resources, monitoring the performance of the corporation, and reporting to the Crown.

In practice, however, the Review has found that none of these authorities has individually been in a position to exercise effective day-to-day supervision over Canada Post. Cumulatively, the effect of being supervised by so many authorities has often been that the corporation is meaningfully supervised by no one.

Ministers responsible for Canada Post have lacked the resources to supervise the corporation on a day-by-day basis. The department supporting the Minister's other responsibilities, Public Works and Government Services, is not the Minister's department for matters pertaining to Canada Post. The Minister's responsibility is personal, not departmental.

Ministers have had some exempt staff capacity to deal with Canada Post, but no real organizational framework. Consequently, if a complaint about the corporation comes into the Minister's office, for instance, Canada Post usually is asked to respond directly or to prepare a reply for the Minister's signature.

> CUMULATIVELY, THE EFFECT OF BEING SUPERVISED BY SO MANY AUTHORITIES HAS OFTEN BEEN THAT THE CORPORATION IS MEANINGFULLY SUPERVISED BY NO ONE.

The President of Treasury Board and the Minister of Finance tend not to involve themselves in Canada Post matters with any frequency or intensity, although there are sometimes exceptions to this. The Crown Corporations Directorate does exercise an ongoing supervisory function, but with limited resources and limited areas of jurisdiction.

The role of Canada Post's Board of Directors has also been much more circumscribed in practice than it is in theory. The Review has found that at least some Board members are convinced that the Board does not play a meaningful role.

In interviews, one Board member told the Review: "We can only hope that CPC Management will recognize that the Board has something to offer."

Another shared the perception that "management sees us as a necessary evil." Another reported that when information is requested on certain issues, "we are often told that it cannot be made available because it is confidential." Yet another said: "CPC management does not think that it is accountable to us."

Based on the above considerations, the Review has reached the following conclusions regarding the governance of Canada Post:

FINDING # 5: **Although Canada Post is owned by the Government, operates on the strength of a monopoly granted by the Government, and is perceived as a representative of the Government in its dealings with Canadians, the corporation is currently beyond any effective control by the Government. None of the authorities entrusted with supervising Canada Post currently have the resources to provide the strong ongoing supervision needed to safeguard the public interest.**

7 Recommendations - Toward a Renewed Canada Post Corporation

Canada's postal service has never been a static institution. Rather, its whole history has been one of change, of evolution, of adaptation to new circumstances. The work of this Review suggests that we have come to a time when change is again needed, to address some significant shortcomings within Canada Post Corporation in the areas of its financial performance, strategic focus, competitive activity, and fundamental public policy responsibilities.

In considering what form that change should take, the Review has been guided by a strong belief that the first principle of government, as it is of medicine, should be: first, do no harm. There is much that is positive and successful about Canada Post as it now stands. It has been no small accomplishment to develop the network and the expertise to deliver the mail everywhere in Canada, despite challenges of geography and climate almost unrivalled in the world. The Review's preoccupation, consequently, has been with seeking ways to preserve and build on the existing strengths of our postal system, while repositioning it sufficiently to overcome current shortcomings and to best meet the needs of Canadians as we move toward the next century.

The range of major strategic approaches suggested to this Review in various submissions has extended all the way from preserving the status quo, to stripping Canada Post of its monopoly or exclusive privilege over lettermail, to establishing a regulatory framework, to privatizing the corporation outright, to removing it from competitive activities. The corporation itself presented in its submission an itemization of nine "requirements" that, in its view, must be met if it is to continue providing universal service at an affordable price. All these suggestions from across Canada have been fully and carefully considered, and the thoughtful work that went into their elaboration is much appreciated.

The criteria against which all the options were tested are threefold:

♦ ensuring that all Canadians get the best possible postal service at an affordable price;

♦ ensuring that the postal needs of Canadian businesses are well met;

♦ ensuring that the functioning of Canada Post is fully consistent with the policy and fiscal priorities of the Government of Canada.

The measures identified as best meeting these tests will not satisfy everyone. In view of the issues involved and the extent to which there are some irreconcilably competing interests, unanimous agreement would probably be impossible under virtually any scenario. The package of suggested changes has been designed with the intention that all interested parties will have at least some of their legitimate concerns met but may also have to bring something to the table in terms of concessions or sacrifice. This balanced approach in the interests of fairness can only be achieved in full, of course, if the Government finds it appropriate to regard the package of recommendations as an integrated whole.

The following sections will examine various key options and make recommendations.

7.1 Universal Service at Uniform Rates

In seeking to define what would constitute the best possible postal services for all Canadians at an affordable price, the Review considered whether Canada Post's current commitments to universality of service and uniformity of price for lettermail are still appropriate and necessary benchmarks.

Neither universal service nor uniform rates are specifically mandated by the Canada Post Corporation Act. The legislation requires only that Canada Post must provide "a basic customary postal service at fair and reasonable rates" and that it must maintain "a standard of service that will meet the needs of the people of Canada and that is similar with respect to communities of the same size."

Nevertheless, Canada Post has submitted to the Review that its first "requirement" is that "CPC must continue to provide universal letter service at affordable, uniform rates." The corporation further states that this is its "central public policy function."[26]

The Review concurs. It has noted that a few submissions - notably from the Competition Bureau and the Fraser Institute - argued that service universality and rate uniformity are economically inefficient. But theoretical economic efficiency, narrowly defined, cannot be a sufficient criterion for sound public policy. From the perspective of the Review, the real-life best interests of Canadians should be the paramount consideration.

Research confirms that postal service continues to play an important role in the lives of an overwhelming majority of Canadians. Roughly 95% of the population sends letters, greeting cards and/or bill payments through the mail, and 84% of Canadians pick up their mail every day.[27] The mail is a particularly important link to the rest of the country and the world for people who live in rural and remote areas - precisely the areas that would most likely be deprived of service in the absence of universality. Since postal service in Canada, as in other countries, continues to constitute a vital public good and a key element of our communications infrastructure, it should be universally available.

With regard to price, similarly, the principle of uniformity is founded on the sound premise that, in a country as far-flung as Canada, people should not be financially penalized in their access to a core federal public service solely by virtue of living elsewhere than in large urban centres. This is distinct from the issue of whether there should be a price differential between *local* mail that is sent and received in the same postal area, and *forward* mail that must be transported greater distances and sorted more than once. The latter is more costly to process, and until 1968 the post office had two stamp prices and even separate mailboxes: one for local mail, the other for inter-city.

---

[26]Canada Post Corporation, *Ensuring Universal Service at Affordable Rates*, op. cit.; page 31.

[27]Quantitative research conducted for the Review by Decima Research; June 1996.

There would be no apparent unfairness in restoring such a two-price system, as long as the difference was solely between local and non/local rather than based on the location of the communities in question. Canada Post's view, however, is that the costs and inefficiencies of managing a local/forward price differential would outweigh any potential revenue benefits. The Review accepts this reasoning.

It is therefore recommended:

> 1.   THAT PROVIDING UNIVERSALITY OF SERVICE AND UNIFORMITY OF PRICE FOR LETTERMAIL BE REGARDED AS INTEGRAL ELEMENTS OF THE MANDATE OF CANADA POST CORPORATION.

> 2.   THAT IN ANY FUTURE AMENDMENTS TO THE CANADA POST CORPORATION ACT, THE OBLIGATION TO PROVIDE UNIVERSAL SERVICE AT A UNIFORM RATE FOR LETTERMAIL BE EXPLICITLY INCLUDED AS PART OF THE CORPORATION'S MANDATE.

7.2 Removing the Exclusive Privilege

Several submissions to the Review - notably from the Competition Bureau, the Fraser Institute and several utility companies - suggested that Canada Post be shorn of its exclusive privilege or monopoly over lettermail.

Canada Post, for its part, cited retention of the exclusive privilege as the second of its "requirements," stating:

> "For as long as it is the public policy of Canada to provide universal letter service at uniform rates, it will be necessary to maintain the limited exclusive privilege for letters. In the near term, the statutory abolition of the exclusive privilege would produce results adverse to the interests of Canadians."[28]

---

[28]Canada Post Corporation, *Ensuring Universal Service at Affordable Rates*, op. cit.; page 32.

While a number of governments have been reviewing the exclusive privilege of their postal services, the Review notes that only three countries in the world - Sweden, Finland and Australia - have abolished it. The circumstances of all three are so different from Canada's that their experience is not applicable.

It is widely accepted in other countries that without exclusive privilege it would be virtually impossible to maintain a universal postal system, let alone one with uniform rates. This is particularly true in a country like Canada, with our great distances and large numbers of sparsely-populated rural communities.

If Canada Post's exclusive privilege were removed, private companies would concentrate on competing in high-density urban areas, perhaps with a special emphasis on local mail. They would ignore rural and remote markets, because the combination of sparse populations, low mail volumes and numerous distribution points is one that offers little prospect of profitability. Because Canada Post's postage rate must blend the cost and revenue requirements of serving both urban and rural areas, and handling both local and forward mail, private firms serving only the most lucrative urban markets would be able to undercut the corporation's rate in those markets and siphon away business.

Canada Post would find its lettermail volumes and revenues reduced, while still having to maintain the same extensive network in order to provide universal service. The eventual result would be dramatically higher postage rates, an end to universal service or, most likely, some combination of both. Even worse, our postal system would be irrevocably fragmented.

To ensure that all Canadians continued to receive postal service, the Government would have to introduce some form of subsidy scheme to permit a financially- weakened Canada Post to continue to serve non-urban areas or to induce private companies to serve them instead. Almost certainly, it would also be necessary to create a new regulatory agency to try to ensure that an increasingly fragmented postal system did not descend into chaos. At best, Canadians would face a very difficult transition period. The long-term results would be impossible to predict.

Removal of the exclusive privilege would be tantamount, in effect, to tossing Canada's postal system up into the air, allowing it to smash into a random assortment of pieces, and hoping that those pieces would somehow re-arrange themselves into a coherent whole that was better or at least as good as the current system.

The suggested removal of the exclusive privilege strikes the Review, in any event, as a solution in search of a problem. Our current postage rate is among the lowest in the world, and even any foreseeable increase would not make the current system prohibitively expensive. It is not at all clear, consequently, why the introduction of competition - whose main theoretical purpose would be to reduce prices - would in this instance be worth all the attendant disruption and risks. Nor is it even clear that the net result would indeed be lower prices, certainly not for all Canadians, everywhere. Similarly, there is no reason to believe that removal of the exclusive privilege would be likely to result in improved postal service for all Canadians.

Given the importance of maintaining the exclusive privilege, the Review notes with concern an apparently growing tendency - notably among municipal governments - to defy that privilege by undertaking their own deliveries. The exclusive privilege is the price we pay for maintaining universal postal service at affordable rates. It exists by the will of Parliament on behalf of the people of Canada.

It follows that no one, let alone other parts of the public sector, should feel entitled to disregard the exclusive privilege at will. Canada Post has not only the right, but the obligation, to defend that privilege by the legal avenues available to it, rather than negotiate compromises which allow it to be eroded.

It is therefore recommended:

> **3.** THAT THE EXCLUSIVE PRIVILEGE OF CANADA POST CORPORATION WITH REGARD TO LETTERMAIL BE MAINTAINED IN ITS CURRENT FORM.

> **4.** THAT THE GOVERNMENT OF CANADA DIRECT CANADA POST CORPORATION TO VIGOROUSLY DEFEND THE EXCLUSIVE PRIVILEGE BY RECOURSE TO APPROPRIATE LEGAL AVENUES, AND THAT THE GOVERNMENT PROVIDE THE CORPORATION WITH ANY NECESSARY SUPPORT IN THAT REGARD.

7.3 Establishing a Regulatory Framework

A significant number of submissions suggested that Canada Post should be made subject to third-party regulation by a body similar to the Canadian Radio-television and Telecommunications Commission (CRTC), the National Energy Board or the National Transportation Agency.

The arguments for regulation initially appear persuasive. A regulatory body could supervise Canada Post's competitive behaviour, establish a financial framework, pass judgment on proposed rate changes, monitor the quality of service, examine proposed involvement in new services, and assess whether specific activities are consistent with the corporation's mandate.

Despite the superficial appeal of such an approach, however, in practice it would be likely to create more problems than it would solve.

The first obstacle is that Canada Post is vehemently opposed to third-party regulation. At the Review's public meeting in Ottawa, the President of the corporation, Mr. Clermont, made it clear that Canada Post would regard a regulatory body as a tool of its competitors:

> "What they want is an American system, one that will tie our hands in such a way that it will give them free reign to capture our markets or at least the

ones that are lucrative and destroy the only Canadian competitor large enough to compete effectively all across our nation."

A previous attempt at third-party regulation of Canada Post in 1988, the Postal Services Review Committee (PSRC) headed by Alan Marchment, failed largely because of precisely this sort of attitude on the part of the corporation. As professor Robert Campbell notes in his book, *The Politics of the Post*:

"CPC was far from happy about the PSRC and regulation, as it had little to gain and much to lose. And it had the power to disrupt the process, which it proceeded to do...CPC (went) on the offensive, challenging the PSRC's authority, vetting its every move, and generally being unhelpful and belligerent. This fractiousness was especially apparent with regard to information...CPC maintained that the requests were unmanageable, outside the committee's mandate, and potentially damaging to its competitive position. In short, CPC refused to provide the information."[29]

It is unlikely, based on its recent statements about regulatory bodies, that the relationship between Canada Post and a new regulatory mechanism would be significantly different. At best, this would create a difficult and troublesome situation from the outset.

Second, existing regulatory processes in Canada have recently not been problem-free. Decisions of the CRTC, for instance, are now almost routinely appealed to the Cabinet. The same pattern would most likely apply to rulings by a regulatory body with regard to Canada Post. That is all the more probable since the corporation would be certain to invoke "commercial sensitivity" in insisting that detailed data on which the rulings were based not be made public. Under the circumstances, creating a new regulatory body - over the vehement objections of the entity it is to regulate - would principally have the effect of adding new controversies and pressures to those already existing in the regulatory field.

Third, the creation of a regulatory framework would require the Government to redefine its relationship with the corporation. At present, the Treasury

---

[29]Robert M. Campbell, *The Politics of the Post*, Broadview press, 1994; page 349.

Board reviews Canada Post's annual corporate plan as prescribed by the Financial Administration Act. A third-party regulatory agency could only complicate this relationship. The Government's rights to direct the corporation as its shareholder and owner could easily come into conflict with the need to maintain an arm's-length approach toward matters subject to regulation. Since the regulatory process itself would not necessarily be fully effective in the absence of willing cooperation by Canada Post, the net result could well be counter-productive.

Fourth, the regulatory process is by its nature time-consuming and costly. Costs would be imposed not only on the Government and the corporation, but also on interested parties wishing to argue a case before the regulatory body. Congressional sources in Washington have told the Review that postal regulation in the United States is only partially effective and fair, because the process is really open only to very powerful interests with large sums of money to spend. In its submission to the Review, the Competition Bureau makes a similar point: "The processes of the U.S. Postal Rate Commission have been judged as expensive, bureaucratic, inefficient and wasteful."

For all these reasons, it is recommended:

> **5.** **THAT THE GOVERNMENT REJECT THIRD-PARTY REGULATION AS AN EFFECTIVE APPROACH TO SUPERVISION OF CANADA POST CORPORATION.**

7.4 Privatizing Canada Post

Outright privatization of Canada Post was not an option that received strong support in submissions made to the Review. However, since several major stakeholders advocated this approach, including the Canadian Chamber of Commerce and the Fraser Institute, it was carefully examined by the Review.

Broadly speaking, the corporation could be privatized with the exclusive privilege or without the exclusive privilege.

If Canada Post were privatized while retaining its exclusive privilege, we would be replacing an unregulated public sector monopoly in unrestrained competition with the private sector, with an unregulated *private* sector monopoly in unrestrained competition with the private sector. It is difficult to see in what sense that would be an improvement. In fact, with the Government losing its right to direct the corporation as its shareholder and proprietor, the only existing control over its activities would be removed.

Since a national private sector postal service would be accountable only to its shareholders and understandably preoccupied solely with maximizing profits, the public interest would be entirely unprotected. The corporation would have every reason to withdraw or reduce service to less profitable areas, and to cease its least lucrative activities. Universality of service as well as uniformity and affordability of pricing would not last long.

The Government would almost certainly have to establish some form of regulatory body to supervise the privatized corporation and ensure that certain basic levels of service were provided at reasonable cost. This would inevitably entail the regulatory problems discussed above. Even then, it would be unrealistic to believe a private corporation would agree to carry out unprofitable activities without the introduction of a subsidy system. To some degree, the Government would be at the financial mercy of this private entity in order to ensure availability of adequate service everywhere in Canada, and it would be drawn back into funding postal services out of general revenues.

At the same time, the privatized entity would no doubt be engaging in aggressive competition with the private sector on the strength of a network previously built up through the outlay of public funds and of a monopoly revenue base conferred by the state. That could only aggravate, not allay, the concerns about competitive fairness detailed in this report.

On the other hand, if Canada Post were privatized without continuation of the exclusive privilege, that would give rise to all the problems discussed above with regard to withdrawing the exclusive privilege. The postal system would be fragmented. A new regulatory agency would still be needed to try to coordinate the provision of services. Subsidies would still be required if more remote and sparsely populated areas were not to be cut off from receiving mail. It is not at all clear how well all this would work, let alone why it would be an improvement on keeping postal service in the public sector.

The Review notes in this regard that, at the public meetings, it asked the presenters from the Fraser Institute and the Canadian Chamber of Commerce how ordinary Canadians - and particularly those in non-urban areas - would benefit from their recommended privatization of Canada Post. They were unable to offer any clear answer. In fact, Dr. Gordon Davies, speaking on behalf of the Fraser Institute, acknowledged: "Some consumers in rural areas may be threatened or may feel threatened by our recommendations."

The Review also notes that even countries with an exceptional enthusiasm for privatization - including Britain, Australia and New Zealand - decided that the postal service was not a good candidate. In Australia, where there is no exclusive privilege, a special industry commission study recommended that Australia Post be privatized by 1997, but the government rejected the proposal. In New Zealand, the post has been restructured to operate according to the rules of business, but it remains a public enterprise. In Britain, the government sought to privatize the Royal Post, but quickly reconsidered when its own backbenchers threatened to bolt the party over the issue. It is noteworthy in this regard that Margaret Thatcher, who perhaps more than anyone else started the wave of privatizations that has swept much of the world since the early 1980s, deliberately kept her distance from privatizing the post office. Rather, she remarked that it is "an integral part of people's lives and most British citizens would be reluctant to see it pass out of government control."[30]

At the level of practicality, any privatization of Canada Post would entail a number of immediate adverse consequences. There is little doubt that, even in the most optimistic scenario, the transition from a public to a private postal system would require a period of adjustment that would disrupt postal services for several years. This would create serious problems for Canadian businesses, which continue to rely heavily on the mail. It is scarcely surprising that very few companies have expressed any enthusiasm for full privatization of the corporation.

---

[30]Facts on File, Library of Parliament, 10 November 1994; page 845.

It is noteworthy, as well, that privatization of postal services might well have a particularly negative impact on women workers. A strikingly large percentage of postmasters and postal assistants are women. For example, out of 6,679 postmasters and assistants, 5,806 or 86.9% were female. Jobs in rural post offices are of special importance to women, because the local economies of rural areas are primarily resource-based and offer them comparatively few employment opportunities. Since privatization would likely lead to numerous closings of rural post offices, the impact on women is a significant consideration.

Beyond narrowly practical matters, the Review gives very considerable emphasis to the national unity implications that any privatization of Canada Post would entail.

Canada Post is by far the most visible federal presence in Canada. It is present everywhere Canadians live, and it serves all Canadians in an essentially non-discriminatory fashion. Canadians rich or poor, in the largest city or the smallest hamlet, all have access to first class mail at the same price and are all fundamentally treated the same. In this sense, the postal service continues to bind Canadians together, as it has from the very day our country was born. The fact that this presence is not currently being used to its full potential does nothing to diminish its inherent importance.

There are ever fewer common services - in effect, common denominators - to which every Canadian can easily relate. Public enterprises have historically played an important role in shaping Canada's identity and cohesion, by contributing to a shared sense of belonging and a shared sense of common purpose. This aspect of our sense of identity has undoubtedly been affected by the recent privatization of such highly visible national institutions as Air Canada, Canadian National and Petro Canada, and by the ongoing reduction of the role of the federal Government in various fields.

There is a limit to our capacity to chip away at the presence and legitimacy of the Government of Canada without adversely affecting social cohesion and national unity. We are probably at that limit, or very close to it. In that context, privatization of Canada Post would be an extremely powerful psychological signal, of the worst possible kind.

If there is any one thing Canadians have always expected their national government to do since the very beginnings of our country, it is to deliver the mail; indeed, one of the main conditions of Prince Edward Island's entry into Confederation was improved postal service. Privatizing Canada Post in today's circumstances, after all the other reductions in the federal role and presence that have taken place, would be tantamount to telling Canadians that their national government can no longer do anything well, not even deliver the mail. Particularly since even the advocates of privatizing Canada Post have been unable to demonstrate that it would bring any real benefits, such a course would make no sense.

It is therefore recommended:

> **6.** **THAT CANADA POST REMAIN A CROWN CORPORATION IN THE PUBLIC SECTOR, AND THAT THE OPTION OF ITS PRIVATIZATION AS AN ENTITY BE REJECTED.**

7.5 Removing Canada Post from Competitive Activities

If Canada Post is to continue to be the face of the Government of Canada in communities across our nation, that face must be benign. This need is not met when such a powerful and important entity of the Government of Canada is engaged in unrestrained competition with private companies. It is not met when the resulting culture of competitive fervour pushes the corporation into such an aggressive posture toward competitors and critics that some Canadians are in fear of retaliation or harassment by an entity of their own Government.

The Review has found that the competitive activities of Canada Post, based as they are on the foundation of the corporation's exclusive privilege and of the network it has built with public funds, are incompatible with basic principles of fairness. It has found that the emphasis on competitive activities has distorted Canada Post's corporate culture and behaviour, diverting it away from a focus on the public service and public policy responsibilities that are the reason for its existence. And it has found that the corporation's strategy of diversifying ever further into competition with the private sector has failed, in any event, to produce good financial results.

The Review has carefully considered all the available options for addressing the problems created by Canada Post's competitive activities outside the scope of its core public policy responsibilities.

Third-party regulation is not a satisfactory solution, due both to Canada Post's emphatic opposition and to the other difficulties it would entail. Regulation would not, moreover, resolve all the problems arising from Canada Post's involvement in competition. Removal of the exclusive privilege and/or privatization would create more problems than would be solved.

The Review has therefore concluded that there is only one approach that would be fully effective while being most consistent with the public interest: a strategic refocussing of Canada Post on its core public policy responsibilities, accompanied by withdrawal from all competitive activities that go beyond those responsibilities.

This is envisaged not as a backward step nor as a negative or punitive one, but rather as a dynamic and positive adjustment to respond to changed circumstances. It should be a cause for satisfaction for the Government of Canada, or for one of its entities, when parts of the private sector have developed sufficiently that they can be left to take over certain activities without in any way imperilling the public interest.

The activities of Canada Post fall into two broad categories. First, there are the core postal services that the private sector could not provide as well in accordance with the principles of universal service and uniform pricing; these are the public policy reason for the corporation's existence. And second, there are the non-core competitive services that the private sector can and does provide; the corporation is involved in these not for any public policy reason, but solely for the revenues they generate. By concentrating exclusively on the first category, Canada Post would be freed to pursue excellence in the services that are the reason for its existence and that it is uniquely able to provide, while avoiding the problems to which its involvement in the second category gives rise.

In summary, Canada Post should withdraw from its competitive activities because:

♦ They place the Government of Canada in an untenable position with regard to fair treatment of the private sector. For understandable reasons related to past behaviour, secretiveness and lack of accountability, there is now no scenario under which private companies will believe that Canada Post is a fair competitor.

♦ They distract Canada Post from concentrating on the pursuit of excellence in the provision of core postal services, and distort its corporate culture by whipsawing it between public service and purely commercial orientation.

♦ They are unnecessary in view of the private sector's now-developed capacity to provide the same services, and therefore they are inconsistent with the Government's determination only to be involved in those activities for which there is a public policy reason.

♦ They are non-essential from a financial point of view, because other options exist to maintain an adequate revenue base for the corporation without the problems that its involvement in competitive activities engenders.

7.5.1 The Canada Post Viewpoint

It is clear that the corporation does not see the matter this way. As its third "requirement" in its submission to the Review, it postulates that "CPC must continue to provide competitive services." In Canada Post's view, it needs the revenues from competitive services to help defray the overhead and other fixed costs of its network. Without those revenues, the corporation believes, it would be unable to provide universal service at uniform, affordable rates.

This is a cogent, internally coherent analysis. Where the Review parts company with the corporation, however, is with regard to Canada Post's insistence that this is the *only* realistically feasible way to operate. As will be detailed below, there are other strategies that can enable the corporation to have the revenues it needs in order to provide its core postal services, while avoiding the drawbacks that its current approach entails.

In support of its view that there is no alternative to remaining involved in competitive services, Canada Post has relied heavily on the report it commissioned from the consulting firm of Coopers & Lybrand, entitled "Choices for a Self-Sustaining Canada Post." The key finding of this report is, in essence, that Canada Post is in such poor financial shape that it would go broke if it were forced to withdraw from competitive activities. The Review had heard considerable debate about the methodology of this report and hence about the credence its findings should be given. In view of the weight that Canada Post has invited the Review and the public to give to this report, the Review commissioned an independent assessment of it by Gordon Ritchie, a former federal deputy minister and deputy chief negotiator of the Canada-U.S. Free Trade Agreement. His principal conclusion is as follows:

> "On the basis of my experience in the strategic direction of public and private corporations, I must tell you that the 'Choices' report does not, in my judgment, constitute a satisfactory basis for making critical judgments about the future of the Canada Post Corporation."

Mr. Ritchie goes on to explain, in part:

> "The failings of the report are inherent in its basic methodology. In any such study, the underlying assumptions obviously influence the results of the various scenarios...I do not find certain of these assumptions compelling. These assumptions are not supported in the report...Second, the analysis is virtually wholly pre-determined by these assumptions, with very little if any informational or analytical value added in the pages of text of the report...The consequence is to transform the 'scenarios' into tautologies. Third, the most important questions and issues are left unexplored in the report...They include such issues as: the elasticity of certain markets with respect to price; the cost savings to be generated through withdrawal from certain markets; and the overall potential opportunities for improved profitability to which there is allusion in the closing sections of the report."

The Review concurs with Mr. Ritchie's independent analysis and accepts it as the Review's own. While the Coopers & Lybrand report presents a noteworthy viewpoint concordant with that of Canada Post, it cannot be regarded as conclusive with regard to the issues under discussion here. The Review's own finding is that there are strategies under which Canada Post can and should withdraw from competitive activities, with no adverse consequences for its financial viability. The Review notes as well that, even accepting at face value the Coopers & Lybrand report's possibly pessimistic projection of annual revenue losses in the range of $200 million a year if Canada Post exits from competitive activities, the strategies to be recommended below would more than make up for that shortfall.

7.5.2 Convergence with Sound Management Practice

While critics of this change, including Canada Post, will undoubtedly perceive it as a nostalgic attempt to "roll back the clock," it is in fact fully consistent with current management theory. We are in an era of corporate downsizing, characterized by recognition that bigger is not necessarily better and that corporations can be most successful by confining themselves to what they do best. As management expert Peter Drucker puts it:

> "Unlike communities, societies, or families, organizations are purposefully designed and always specialized...An organization is defined by its task. The symphony orchestra does not attempt to cure the sick; it plays music. The hospital takes care of the sick but does not attempt to play Beethoven. Indeed, an organization is effective only if it concentrates on one task. Diversification destroys the performance capacity of an organization, whether it is a business, a labour union, a school, a hospital, a community service or a house of worship ...An organization is a tool. And as with any other tool, the more specialized it is, the greater its capacity to perform its given task."[31]

---

[31]Peter F. Drucker, *Managing in a Time of Great Change*; Truman Talley Books/Dutton, New York, 1995; page 85.

Exiting from competitive activities will enable Canada Post to enhance its specialization and hence increase its effectiveness. In recent years, the corporation has increasingly been torn between providing a public service and functioning as a competitive commercial business. In addition to its given task of delivering the mail, it has taken on a distracting array of other tasks: functioning as a courier company, competing as a provider of unaddressed admail, operating business support centres, experimenting with electronic communications, and so on.

Refocussing on its fundamental task of providing core postal services would therefore constitute a strategically progressive step forward for the corporation, a step fully consistent with the most contemporary management theories.

7.5.3 Convergence with the Government's Policy Direction

In the 1995 federal Budget, the Minister of Finance, Mr. Martin, stated:

> "The Government is committed to privatizing and commercializing government operations wherever feasible and appropriate. Our view is straightforward. If the Government does not need to run something, it should not, and in the future it will not."

It is a finding of the Review that Canada Post's competitive activities fall squarely into the category of what the Government "does not need to run" and therefore, in accordance with Government policy, should not. In each case - specifically including courier services, commercial unaddressed admail, business support or mailing centres, and electronic products and services - there is a vibrant private sector capable of doing the job and, in fact, already engaged in doing it.

Canada Post has suggested to the Review that since it operates as an integrated business, the Budget statement should apply only to the corporation as a whole, rather than to its individual activities. It is difficult to believe this suggestion was meant seriously. The Government's Program Review process has by no means been confined to scrutinizing departments only in their entirety. On the contrary, specific activities and programs are assessed with regard to their continuing appropriateness and necessity. It is impossible to see why a different standard would apply to Canada Post, particularly since its activities are *not* inseparable.

In fact, the Review thought it useful to apply the Government's six Program Review tests to the corporation's competitive activities. These are the results:

♦ **Public Interest Test - Does the program area or activity continue to serve a public interest?**
No. Courier services, commercial unaddressed admail, business support centres and electronic products and services are all activities that serve no public policy objective. They are purely commercial, private sector activities.

♦ **Role of Government Test - Is there a legitimate and necessary role for government in this program area or activity?**
No. There is no legitimate or necessary role for government or one of its entities in providing courier services, delivering unaddressed admail (which also entails adverse environmental consequences), running business support centres or providing electronic products and services. These are all activities that can be, and are being, carried out by the private sector.

♦ **Federalism Test - Is the current role of the federal government appropriate, or is the program a candidate for realignment with the provinces?**
Not applicable. While the postal service is and should remain under federal jurisdiction, the particular activities in question are not appropriate for *any* level of government. They have no public policy objectives and are purely commercial in nature.

♦ **Partnership Test - What activities or programs should or could be transferred in whole or in part to the private/voluntary sector?**
All the competitive activities in question can and should be

transferred , in whole, to the private sector. They have no public policy rationale, and there is no need for the public sector to be providing them.

♦ **Efficiency Test - If the program or activity continues, how could its efficiency be improved?**
Not applicable. These activities need not continue to be in the public sector. The efficiency of Canada Post with regard to its core public policy responsibilities can be improved, however, by having it transfer its competitive activities to the private sector and concentrate on those core responsibilities.

♦ **Affordability Test - Is the resultant package of programs and activities affordable within the fiscal constraint? If not, what programs or activities would be abandoned?**
Yes. The withdrawal of Canada Post from competitive activities is affordable, because the resulting loss of revenues can be counter-balanced by other measures. No financial burden will result for the Government.

It is therefore a finding of the Review that the withdrawal of Canada Post from competitive activities is not only consistent with the Government's policy direction, but is required by it.

7.5.4 Competitive Areas to be Vacated

As a general principle, Canada Post should no longer engage in competition with the private sector in areas outside its core postal service mandate.

Specifically, that means exiting from the courier business, from unaddressed admail, from the operation of business support or mailing centres, from electronic products and services, and from retailing of non-postal merchandise.

With regard to exiting from the courier business, some precision of definition is appropriate. Clearly, Canada Post should divest itself of Purolator. Beyond that, however, the Review recognizes that a distinction can be made between expedited mail, which is reasonable for the post office to provide, and courier services per se.

In its presentation to the Review, the Canadian Courier Association suggested the following dividing line: what is brought to a post office or retail outlet or deposited in a receptacle or "street furniture" is mail, while what is picked up from a business or residence falls under the category of courier activity. The Review accepts this definition as being restrained and not unduly onerous for the corporation.

While Canada Post could meet this definition by eliminating the pick-up component from Priority Courier, the corporation may take the view that the resulting decrease in volumes would make this product line unprofitable. If Canada Post prefers to exit Priority Courier outright, that would not be problematic from the Review's standpoint. The possibility was incorporated in the Review's analysis of the financial implications of removing Canada Post from competitive activities.

Disallowing Canada Post from providing pick-up service will remove it from direct competition with courier companies, without significantly affecting its ability to exploit cost economies of scale and scope within its existing lettermail network. Since point-to-point service usually requires a separate dedicated visit to pick up the product, eliminating pick-up service should not significantly affect the corporation's ability to leverage the network and operate efficiently. As well, Canada Post might offset volume declines in its network by putting more emphasis on improving delivery standards and marketing for Xpresspost, which is generally dropped off by the customer.

In the case of unaddressed admail, there is one aspect that does fall within Canada Post's public policy responsibilities. It is desirable that governments - municipal, provincial and federal - and their elected members should have a way of reaching the public for informational purposes. Canada Post's public policy role and universal reach make it logical for it to continue playing a role in that regard. Therefore, unaddressed mail from governments and elected members should be exempted from Canada Post's withdrawal from unaddressed admail.

Electronic products and services present a set of issues somewhat different from those raised by other non-core services in which Canada Post is involved. With the exception of remote desktop publishing, the problem is not so much that the corporation is engaged in aggressive competition with the private sector as that it appears to be devoting attention, money and human resources to a field in which it has no particular expertise or credibility and in which it has identified no clear markets for itself.

For this reason, while including electronic products and services in the list of activities from which Canada Post should exit, the Review adds the following qualification: in the event that the corporation identifies any electronic product or service that meets a demonstrable public policy need and that the private sector is unable or unwilling to provide in a way that would adequately serve the public interest, Canada Post should be able to apply to the government for permission to provide that specific product or service. Such permission should be granted only if the corporation is able to clearly demonstrate a need, its unique ability to meet that need, an identifiable market for the product or service, and a coherent strategy for proceeding.

Based on all the foregoing considerations, it is therefore recommended:

> **7.** THAT THE GOVERNMENT DIRECT CANADA POST CORPORATION TO WITHDRAW FROM ALL COMPETITION WITH THE PRIVATE SECTOR IN AREAS OF ACTIVITY OUTSIDE ITS CORE PUBLIC POLICY RESPONSIBILITIES FOR PROVIDING POSTAL SERVICES.

> **8.** THAT THE GOVERNMENT SPECIFICALLY DIRECT CANADA POST CORPORATION TO DIVEST ITSELF OF PUROLATOR COURIER AT FAIR MARKET VALUE AND TO WITHDRAW FROM ALL OTHER COURIER SERVICES, WHICH ARE DEFINED AS SERVICES INVOLVING PICK-UP OF THE ENVELOPE OR PARCEL FROM A BUSINESS OR RESIDENTIAL ADDRESS.

> **9.** THAT THE GOVERNMENT SPECIFICALLY DIRECT CANADA POST CORPORATION TO WITHDRAW FROM ALL UNADDRESSED ADMAIL SERVICES, WITH THE EXCEPTION OF UNADDRESSED MATERIALS FROM THE MUNICIPAL, PROVINCIAL AND FEDERAL LEVELS OF GOVERNMENT AND THEIR ELECTED MEMBERS, WHICH THE CORPORATION SHOULD CONTINUE TO DELIVER AS PART OF ITS PUBLIC POLICY RESPONSIBILITIES.

> **10.** THAT THE GOVERNMENT SPECIFICALLY DIRECT CANADA POST CORPORATION TO WITHDRAW FROM PROVIDING ELECTRONIC PRODUCTS AND SERVICES, SUBJECT TO THE FOLLOWING PROVISO: IF THE CORPORATION IDENTIFIES A SPECIFIC PRODUCT OR SERVICE THAT MEETS A DEMONSTRABLE PUBLIC POLICY NEED AND THAT THE PRIVATE SECTOR IS UNABLE OR UNWILLING TO PROVIDE IN A WAY THAT MEETS THE PUBLIC INTEREST, THE CORPORATION MAY APPLY TO THE GOVERNMENT FOR PERMISSION TO OFFER THAT ELECTRONIC PRODUCT OR SERVICE.

7.6 Costs of Withdrawing from Competitive Activities

The recommendation to remove Canada Post from competitive areas outside its core public policy responsibilities is founded on a financial strategy to ensure that the corporation can accomplish this withdrawal without impeding its ability to provide universal lettermail service at a uniform, affordable price.

This strategy has two components: analysis of the initial costs and ongoing revenue impact of exiting from competitive products and services, and identification of appropriate ways to offset those financial consequences. It must be emphasized that, due to the limitations of the information available to the Review, the following calculations necessarily are order-of-magnitude estimates rather than formal forecasts of actual results.

The financial effects of withdrawing from competitive activities can be broken down into two main categories.

The first category includes the initial costs of exiting these products. These costs would include the cost of reducing staff (buyouts, severance packages, outplacement counselling, etc.), redesigning the network (revising routes, transferring remaining employees, retraining, etc.), closing facilities (lease buyouts, decommissioning, relocation, etc.), disposing of or redeploying surplus assets, and the write-off of investments. In addition, it appears likely that network redesign may not be completed before products are exited. Accordingly, an estimate was made of costs which might continue to be incurred for a portion of the first year after the products are exited and the corporation has ceased to earn revenue from those products.

The second category of costs includes the ongoing or annual impact of exiting product lines after the initial, first-year costs are incurred. These ongoing costs represent the lost contribution to common network costs.

7.6.1 Initial Exit Costs

The Review used three different methods of estimating the combined total of these initial exit costs and additional wind-up costs. The result is an estimated total exit cost range of between $504 and $579 million.

The Review has assumed that Canada Post could fund these exit costs through borrowing. It has further assumed that the cost of interest on the borrowed money, plus an approximation of the amounts to be repaid, would add to the "losses" the corporation would incur by ceasing to be involved in competitive activities. For ease of calculation, and to best capture the level of returns needed by Canada Post to cover the financial impacts of withdrawal, it is assumed that any funds borrowed will be repaid in blended interest and principal payments over the term of the borrowing. It is assumed for these calculations that the corporation would borrow the full initial exit and wind-up costs, less cash balances of $59 million at March 30 1996, at 8% for a term of 20 years. Based on these assumptions, Canada Post's annual cash requirements to pay interest and principal on this "exit debt" would range from $45 million to $53 million.

7.6.2 Ongoing Contribution Losses and Costs

In calculating the ongoing annual impact of withdrawing from competitive activities, the Review has used product contribution figures from the 1994/95 Canada Post Corporation Annual Cost Study, revised to reflect the impact of the allocation to product lines of the $180 million that the Review found Canada Post had incorrectly failed to allocate.

Again using three methodologies, the Review estimates that the combined negative financial impact of foregone contributions (product revenues minus costs) and borrowing costs would range between $80 million and $121 million. This is considerably less than the negative impact of $200 million a year, even without borrowing to cover initial exit costs, estimated by the Coopers & Lybrand report. Even in the somewhat unlikely event that the more pessimistic Coopers & Lybrand calculations are more accurate, however, revenue strategies identified by the Review would suffice to cover those impacts.

7.7 Revenue Strategies

As emphasized above, the withdrawal of Canada Post from competitive activities is envisaged not as a negative step, but as a strategic repositioning to enable the corporation to better serve Canadians by concentrating on the pursuit of excellence in its core public policy postal functions.

For this repositioning to be successful, it is essential that the financial stability of the corporation be strengthened, not weakened. Therefore - guided by the principles of fairness, priority concern for the public interest, continued affordability of postal services, and compatibility with the policy direction of the Government - the Review has identified several revenue strategies to achieve this objective.

7.7.1 Postage Rates

Canada currently has the second lowest basic postage rate in the industrialized world (Table 5). No one likes rate increases, and the

Review fully recognizes that the business community is particularly concerned about keeping postage rates as low as possible.

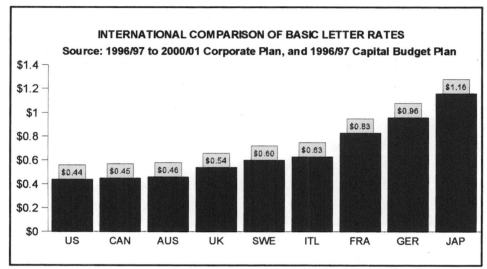

INTERNATIONAL COMPARISON OF BASIC LETTER RATES
Source: 1996/97 to 2000/01 Corporate Plan, and 1996/97 Capital Budget Plan

Table 5

Nevertheless, the Review is also aware of significant levels of dissatisfaction with the reliability and speed of the mail; with some aspects of service, particularly with regard to community mailboxes; and, particularly among businesses, with the unpredictability of price increases. If Canadians are assured value for their money, in terms of a refocussing of Canada Post on the pursuit of excellence and reliability in its core services - as will be recommended below - the Review is of the belief that they would accept a reasonable one-time increase to make this possible.

The Review also believes that Canadians will agree that it makes no sense to underprice our postage rate to such an extent that Canada Post is driven to compete inappropriately with private businesses in an attempt to make ends meet.

Quantitative and qualitative opinion analysis conducted for the Review by Decima Research leads to the conclusion that Canadians would accept an increase in the basic postal rate to 50 cents as not being unduly burdensome, and that they would not dramatically change their use of the postal system as a result. There is a strong expectation, however, with which the Review concurs, that such an increase should be accompanied by a commitment to improved postal service.

If a 5-cent rate increase were applied across the board, it could generate an estimated $175 million a year in additional revenues for Canada Post, taking into account extrapolated impact on volumes.

There could be an argument, however, for increasing the rate for Incentive Lettermail and Addressed Admail by 10% rather than a flat 5 cents, to avoid distorting the price differential between these discounted products and regular lettermail. In that event, the total additional revenues generated by the rate increase would be not $175 million but an estimated $140 million.

In the judgment of the Review, this increase in the basic postal rate is inescapably necessary.

It is therefore recommended:

> **11.** THAT THE FIRST-CLASS POSTAGE RATE BE INCREASED TO **50** CENTS, AND THAT THIS INCREASE BE ACCOMPANIED BY A COMMITMENT TO FURTHER IMPROVEMENT OF CORE POSTAL SERVICES.

7.7.2 Contribution from Courier Services

The obvious beneficiary of Canada Post's withdrawal from the courier industry will be all private sector courier companies. The courier industry has been emphatic in telling the Review that its member companies have suffered substantial volume and revenue impacts as a result of Canada Post's competitive activities. It therefore follows that the corporation's cessation of those activities should be highly profitable for private companies.

But the Review notes that the withdrawal of Canada Post from competitive activities in its field is not something to which the courier industry is *entitled*; it is merely appropriate public policy under the circumstances that have developed. The Review further notes that the private sector courier industry is only able to operate in Canada at all, in the face of Canada Post's exclusive privilege, by virtue of several provisions in the Canada Post Corporation Act that effectively give its activities an exception from that exclusive privilege.

It seems fair, therefore, that in exchange for having Canada Post vacate the courier field in their favour, the courier companies should bring a contribution of their own to the table in order to prevent Canada Post - and the public interest - from suffering undue losses as a result.

The form that such a contribution should most appropriately take is suggested by a provision of Section 601 of the U.S. Postal Administration Act which provides, among other requirements, that in the United States "A letter may be carried out of the mails when...the amount of postage which would have been charged on the letter if it had been sent by mail is paid by stamps, or postage meter stamps," on the envelope. In practice, however, most major U.S. courier companies operate under an alternative provision, Section 320.6 which states that "extremely urgent" letters may be carried out of the mail provided the amount paid for private carriage is at least three dollars or twice the applicable U.S. postage for first class mail, whichever is greater.

Courier companies in Canada currently operate by virtue of a similar "multiple-of-postage" provision for "letters of an urgent nature" in Section 15 of the Canada Post Corporation Act. Under the circumstances of Canada Post's withdrawal from the courier field, it would be appropriate to provide the corporation with compensatory protection for its revenue base by introducing a provision similar to Section 601 - not as an alternative to the "urgent nature" provision, but as an additional condition to it.

In other words, all courier products would have to have affixed to them a first-class postage stamp, namely a 50-cent stamp if the recommendation of the Review in that regard is accepted. In order to encourage the courier companies to absorb the cost of this contribution rather than pass it on to consumers, and to avoid raising courier rates unduly, Section 15 of the Canada Post Corporation Act should be amended to provide that the fee for "letters of an urgent nature" - *including* the value of an affixed first-class stamp - must be "at least three times the regular rate of postage payable for delivery in Canada of similarly addressed letters weighing fifty grams."

It should be noted that what is envisaged is *not* a "dedicated tax." No revenues would be collected or distributed by the Government. Rather, it is simply a modification in the application of Canada Post's exclusive privilege, and revenues would flow to the corporation in the normal way: through sales of postage.

The Review estimates that requiring all courier products to carry a 50-cent stamp would generate for Canada Post additional revenues of between $209 million and $257 million, depending on what estimate of the size of the courier market is used.

In the opinion of the Review, the withdrawal of Canada Post from the courier industry and the application of the stamp requirement should be inextricably linked - otherwise the courier industry would benefit unduly while the corporation would suffer potentially significant losses.

It is therefore recommended:

> **12.** **THAT, IN EXCHANGE FOR CANADA POST CORPORATION'S WITHDRAWAL FROM COMPETITION IN THE COURIER MARKET, THE COURIER INDUSTRY BE REQUIRED TO MAKE A COMPENSATORY CONTRIBUTION TO THE CORPORATION'S REVENUES, IN THE FORM OF A REQUIREMENT THAT ALL COURIER SHIPMENTS MUST HAVE AFFIXED TO THEM A FIRST-CLASS POSTAGE STAMP.**

7.7.3 Tax or Levy on Unaddressed Admail

By a similar process of reasoning, the Government might want to consider imposing a modest tax or levy on unaddressed admail in conjunction with Canada Post's withdrawal from the field.

There are several possible rationales for such a tax. First, as in the case of the contribution from courier companies, it could be used to compensate Canada Post for revenues foregone by vacating the field of unaddressed admail. Second, to the extent that unaddressed admail is both an environmental problem and a nuisance to those who do not welcome receiving it, a modest tax might reduce its cost-efficiency sufficiently to encourage some advertisers to seek less problematic modes of communication. The Government could also, if it wished, explore earmarking a portion of the revenues from this tax for environmental purposes, as at least a symbolic response to the environmental implications of unaddressed admail.

Unlike the case of the courier industry contribution, Canada Post would not be able to directly collect or access the revenues from this tax. The Government would have to impose and collect the tax itself, and then give Canada Post an appropriation from general revenues - perhaps toward a specified public policy purpose, such as providing enhanced service to elderly or disabled persons in areas served by community mailboxes.

The Review has not done detailed analytical work with regard to the feasibility, methodology or cost/benefits of collecting such a tax. It is estimated, however, that a tax or levy of 5 percent could generate potential additional revenues of $50 million to $100 million.

It is therefore recommended:

> **13.** **THAT THE GOVERNMENT EXPLORE THE MERITS OF LEVYING A MODEST SPECIAL TAX ON UNADDRESSED ADMAIL TO INDIRECTLY COMPENSATE CANADA POST CORPORATION FOR REVENUES FOREGONE BY WITHDRAWING FROM THIS FIELD, AND PERHAPS ALSO TO COUNTER-BALANCE NEGATIVE ENVIRONMENTAL IMPLICATIONS OF UNADDRESSED ADMAIL.**

7.8 Labour Costs

In their presentations to the Review, the Canadian Union of Postal Workers (CUPW) and the other postal unions have shown a thoughtful concern for the public interest and for providing the best possible postal service. The Review does not doubt that CUPW in particular, as by far the largest union, has in recent years made a serious effort to contribute to an improved labour relations climate at the corporation.

It is equally clear from CUPW's presentations and from extensive discussions with the union's leadership, however, that its absolute priority in its dealings with Canada Post is the maximization of employment for its membership on the best possible terms. This is a normal stance for a labour union. But it would be appropriate for it to be counterbalanced in this instance, to a greater extent than is currently apparent, by a recognition that changing circumstances require new approaches - not always in the direction of more jobs at ever more favourable levels of compensation.

The Review notes that both CUPW and Canada Post have, at various times in the course of its work, urged it not to involve itself too deeply in collective bargaining issues. This is advice which the Review readily accepts, particularly since it has lacked the time and resources to explore the complex issues involved in the depth they would deserve.

Canada Post has nevertheless presented detailed information in support of its view that total compensation, particularly with regard to pay for time not worked, is out of line with the private sector and with postal administrations in other countries, and that other provisions with regard to job security and the deployment of its workforce deny it the necessary degree of flexibility. The corporation has calculated that approximately $300 million a year could be saved if wages and benefits were brought into line with those of comparable workers in the private sector.

CUPW has responded in some detail, but its response does not, in the opinion of the Review, constitute a total rebuttal. Aside from disputing specifics of various reports and calculations submitted by the corporation, the union's argument is in essence that it negotiated its extraordinary benefits and work conditions in lieu of higher wages, and that therefore, by definition, these provisions cannot be considered excessive.

The Review cannot agree. The basic reason that labour-management contracts are negotiated to be in effect for a specific period, rather than in perpetuity, is that circumstances change over time within and around each organization. While calculations may differ in quantifying the excesses in contractual arrangements at Canada Post, it appears beyond doubt that key aspects of these arrangements are out of step with the new realities of today's workplace.

There is no readily apparent reason, for instance, why Canada Post workers should enjoy virtually unconditional job security when it is not available to other Canadians in the public or private sectors. Nor is it clear why, for instance, in today's economic environment, letter carriers should have the absolute right to travel to and from their base on the corporation's time for their lunch break, even in some instances by paid taxi. Most Canadians would undoubtedly also be of the view that it is reasonable to expect a full day's work for a full day's pay, a practice which is often not the case under current agreements at Canada Post.

The Review commissioned an independent assessment of available information in this regard by George V. Orser, a former Deputy Secretary of the Staff Relations Branch at the Treasury Board Secretariat. He concluded, in part:

> "Settlements higher than the post office (and others) found desirable were often arrived at either voluntarily or by Government decision to achieve some modicum of labour peace. Money derived from postal revenue and Government appropriations was always available to pay the increased labour costs. The post office, for most of the time it has existed, has not had to compete for its core business. Thus, the totality of pressures which exist in a company engaged in a wholly competitive business were not present. The absence in the past of the competitive pressures which make it imperative to control labour costs has no doubt resulted in compensation levels in CPC which are higher than they would otherwise have been."

Gordon Ritchie, a former federal Deputy Minister and Deputy Chief Negotiator of the Canada-U.S. Free Trade Agreement, in an independent evaluation of Canada Post's financial position for the Review, reached a similar conclusion:

> "The Canadian Union of Postal Workers has been remarkably successful over the past 30 years in arrogating to its members the lion's share of economic rents from the Canada Post monopoly....The existing Canada Post Corporation collective agreements constitute what is arguably the most uncompetitive and inefficient labour agreement currently in place in any jurisdiction in North America...
>
> It should be noted that excessive wages are not the main problem. Pay for time not worked is an even more substantial direct cost burden. The most costly provisions over the long run are probably those restricting the Canada Post Corporation's ability to terminate, to redeploy or to employ more efficiently its huge workforce."

Particularly since labour costs - including wages and benefits, employment levels and job security, and negotiated work practices - account for an estimated total of approximately 75% of Canada Post's operating costs, no strategic repositioning of the corporation can fail to address these issues. If Canada Post is to withdraw from competitive activities as this Review recommends, it must have the flexibility to adjust and redeploy its work force accordingly; these adjustments and redeployments should be conducted in the fairest manner possible and with maximum consideration for the corporation's employees. And if Canada Post is to have access through public policy to new sources of revenue to compensate for the consequences of withdrawing from competition, these revenues should be used to improve service to the Canadian public - not to perpetuate working conditions not available to any other Canadians.

Since the current collective agreement at Canada Post expires July 31, 1997, the imminent round of negotiations on a new agreement provides a crucial opportunity to address these issues. While CUPW and the other postal unions cannot be expected to be enthusiastic about changes they would understandably regard as unfavourable, the Review most strongly suggests to both CUPW and Canada Post that it is in everyone's best interests that a more realistic set of arrangements be negotiated through a process of bargaining in good faith, illuminated by an understanding of the new realities of the Canadian workplace.

It is questionable whether Canada Post could withstand a prolonged work stoppage. The immediate financial consequences could be devastating and there is a very real risk that mail volumes would be irretrievably lost to alternative means of communication. Postal workers would ultimately be imperilling their own livelihood. But this cannot, in the judgment of the Review, be a reason to permit currently inappropriate contractual provisions to remain unchanged. In the worst case scenario, it would be essential for the Government to meet its responsibilities and do what was necessary both to protect the immediate public interest and to ensure a financially sound future for a strategically repositioned Canada Post. But there need be no reason for it to come to that.

CUPW made a persuasive and thoughtful argument in its presentations to the Review, for various improvements to postal services. The best outcome for Canada Post's workers would be to negotiate a more reasonable and contemporary collective agreement, permitting the money saved by the corporation to go toward service improvements that would benefit the Canadian public while maximizing employment opportunities at the corporation.

Without attempting to judge the merits of various competing calculations, it appears to the Review from available information that a minimum of between $100 million and $200 million a year can be saved without subjecting

Canada Post workers to unfair hardships or unreasonable wage rollbacks, merely by bringing contractual provisions into line with the reality experienced by other Canadians.

It is therefore recommended:

> **14.** THAT THE GOVERNMENT DIRECT CANADA POST CORPORATION TO BRING ITS LABOUR COSTS UNDER THE COLLECTIVE AGREEMENT INTO LINE WITH THE REALITIES OF THE CONTEMPORARY CANADIAN WORKPLACE, THROUGH GOOD-FAITH BARGAINING IN THE 1997 CONTRACT NEGOTIATIONS.

> **15.** THAT IN THE EVENT OF A FAILURE OF THE COLLECTIVE BARGAINING PROCESS TO ACHIEVE THE NECESSARY ADJUSTMENTS WITHOUT SERVICE DISRUPTION, THE GOVERNMENT BE PREPARED TO TAKE APPROPRIATE ACTION TO PROTECT THE IMMEDIATE PUBLIC INTEREST AND ENSURE THE LONG-TERM FINANCIAL SOUNDNESS OF A STRATEGICALLY REPOSITIONED CANADA POST CORPORATION.

7.9 Net Financial Implications of Strategic Repositioning

As discussed above, the Review estimates that withdrawing from competitive activities would cost Canada Post between $80 million and $120 million annually in foregone contributions and the cost of borrowing to cover initial exit costs. The Coopers & Lybrand report, with which Canada Post concurs but which the Review regards as overly pessimistic, stated that withdrawing from competitive activities would cost the corporation $200 million a year in foregone revenues. Since that figure does not include the cost of borrowing to cover initial exit costs, an additional $50 million - already included in the Review's calculation above - must be added to the Coopers & Lybrand calculation. Thus, the very worst-case scenario using the Coopers & Lybrand calculation and adding borrowing costs would be approximately $250 million a year.

Thus the range of negative financial consequences for Canada Post from the withdrawal portion of a strategic repositioning would be between $80 million and $250 million. The Review considers the upper reaches of that range to be unrealistically high, but includes them here to ensure that all possible contingencies are covered.

On the revenue side of the repositioning equation, the Review has calculated that a 5-cent increase in basic postal rates would bring the corporation $140 million to $175 million a year. Imposing a first-class stamp requirement on courier shipments would bring between $210 million and $275 million. A 5% tax on unaddressed admail, should the Government choose to impose it, would generate revenues of $50 million to $100 million.

POTENTIAL ADDITIONAL REVENUE		
	$ million low	$ million high
5-cent increase in basic postal rates	140	175
First class stamp on courier shipments	210	275
Subtotal	350	450
5% tax on unaddressed admail	50	100
Total potential revenues	400	550

Table 6

Combined, these three measures would give Canada Post incremental revenues of $400 million to $550 million. If the Government chose not to tax unaddressed admail, the revenue from the first two measures alone would be $350 million to $450 million.

In the most limited revenue scenario, consequently, the incremental revenues of $350 million a year from a postage rate increase and a stamp requirement on courier shipments would be more than enough to offset the Coopers & Lybrand worst-case projection of annual losses totalling $250 million.

In addition to this, the Review has suggested, as discussed above, that necessary adjustments in the collective agreement to bring it into line with the realities of the workplace should save the corporation *at least* another $100 million a year. These savings would not start being realized until late 1997 at the earliest, however.

To all these calculations must be added several other positive financial considerations. First, Canada Post would derive income from the sale of Purolator, with or without Priority Courier, and of any other assets that would become surplus with the exit from competitive activities. Second, withdrawal from competition with the private sector and a renewed focus on its core activities should enable the corporation to reduce costs further by tightening its operations and organizational structures. There would be no need, to cite just one example, for most corporate sponsorships or for such amenities as private boxes at sports facilities.

These calculations are necessarily broadly directional rather than precise, due to the number of variables involved and the limitations on available information. But they indicate to the satisfaction of the Review that the strategic repositioning recommended here would enable Canada Post, under any scenario, to cover the costs of withdrawing from competitive activities and to focus additional resources on improving its core postal services.

7.10 Financial Relationship with the Government

One of the questions put to the Review in its Terms of Reference is whether Canada Post should seek to generate a commercial return on equity or operate on a break-even basis. The answer is implicit in the strategic repositioning recommended by this Review.

Canada Post should be financially self-sustaining. That means generating sufficient revenues to cover its operating costs, capital investment needs and expansions of the core postal service, and the setting aside of financial reserves to cover any difficult years. But since the corporation's focus should be on functioning as a public service with regard to its core postal responsibilities, rather than on operating as a commercial business in competition with the private sector, it follows that it should not be required to generate a full commercial rate of return on equity. The only operational reason for Canada Post to need a commercial rate of return would be to enable the corporation to borrow independently on open markets. Rather, the Government can and should continue to guarantee Canada Post's borrowing, while requiring that the corporation meet specified public policy and performance requirements.

The concentration on a public policy role for the corporation is not consistent, in the opinion of the Review, with expecting it to pay dividends to the Government. The value of such dividends, relative to the overall scale of the Government's financial operations, would be small in any event. But the more important consideration is that, from the viewpoint of this Review, it need not be a priority for the Government to earn a financial return from the provision of what should be regarded as a vital public service.

It would make little policy sense in this context for Canada Post to pay dividends to the Government at the inevitable expense of either having postal rates higher than they would otherwise be, or having correspondingly less money to spend on providing Canadians with the best possible postal services.

At the same time, however, in the absence of the discipline imposed by being required to operate efficiently enough to generate commercial returns on equity and pay dividends, it is essential that there be other strong mechanisms of supervision in place to ensure that the public interest is optimally served and that revenues are not squandered by the corporation. Such mechanisms will be suggested in later sections of this report.

It is therefore recommended:

> **16.** THAT CANADA POST CORPORATION BE MANDATED TO OPERATE ON A BREAK-EVEN BASIS RATHER THAN PURSUE A COMMERCIAL RATE OF RETURN ON EQUITY, AND THAT THIS BREAK-EVEN BASIS BE DEFINED AS GENERATING SUFFICIENT REVENUES TO COVER OPERATING COSTS, APPROPRIATE CAPITAL INVESTMENTS, EXPANSIONS AND IMPROVEMENTS OF CORE POSTAL SERVICES, AND THE SETTING ASIDE OF FINANCIAL RESERVES TO PROTECT AGAINST REVENUE SHORTFALLS IN FINANCIALLY DIFFICULT YEARS.

7.11 Reinforced Federal Identity

The entire rationale for keeping Canada Post in the public sector and having it concentrate on its core postal responsibilities is founded on the importance of the corporation's public policy role and on its value and potential as a nationwide federal presence. Although 82% of Canadians agree with the concept that the post office is an important Federal Government presence in a community[32], Canada Post is now being perceived less as a government presence and more as an independent corporation.

It follows, therefore, that the clarity and vigour of that presence should be reinforced. The new Chairman of Canada Post, Andre Ouellet, who as Postmaster-General presided over its creation as a Crown corporation, has in the past shown a great understanding of the importance of its role as a federal presence. When the corporation was being established, Mr. Ouellet said:

> "In villages and small towns across Canada, the Post Office remains one of the most frequently visited places...The Post Office has over the years become a much needed resource centre...the Post Office is a meeting place for all and creates a bond between members of the community. It is a unifying force which gives one the feeling of belonging...In many places the Post Office was the only representative of the Canadian government. In many villages, the Canadian flag floats at the end of the pole in front of the Post Office and may be the only sign of the federal presence...We urge the Crown corporation to maintain and reflect a corporate identity as an institution of the Government of Canada."[33]

Regrettably, the corporation has not heeded the urging of its then-creator and current Chairman. Instead, as discussed earlier in this report, it has adopted a deliberate strategy of distancing itself as much as possible from any perception that it is part of the Government of Canada.

---

[32]Quantitative research conducted for the Review by Decima Research; June 1996.

[33]Quoted in *The Politics of the Post*, op. cit.; page 19.

It may well be, as Canada Post believes, that private companies are mistrustful of the ability of a public enterprise to efficiently meet their needs. But if the private sector does not believe that an entity of the Government of Canada can provide good service, the appropriate solution is not for that entity to disguise its ownership; it is to provide excellent service.

As part of the recommended strategic refocussing on its public policy responsibilities, Canada Post should reclaim its federal identity in all available ways. It is a good first step that the corporation has restored the Canadian flag to its street furniture since late 1993, at the behest of the Government. But it is not sufficient. Canada Post should restore the Canadian flag insignia, (the Canada wordmark), to all vehicles, signs, advertisements, and all other places where its corporate identity is expressed. Apart from clearly identifying Canada Post to all Canadians as part of the federal presence, this would have the highly desirable effect of constantly reminding the corporation's employees at every level that they represent the Government of Canada in all their activities and should act accordingly.

It is therefore recommended:

> **17.** THAT THE GOVERNMENT DIRECT CANADA POST CORPORATION TO REASSERT ITS IDENTITY AS PART OF THE FEDERAL PRESENCE IN ALL AVAILABLE WAYS, AND SPECIFICALLY BY RESTORING THE CANADIAN FLAG INSIGNIA, (THE CANADA WORDMARK), TO ALL ITS VEHICLES, SIGNS, ADVERTISEMENTS AND ALL OTHER PLACES WHERE ITS CORPORATE IDENTITY IS EXPRESSED.

7.12 Rural Post Office Closings and Service Issues

The Review received strong expressions of concern from Canadians in rural areas about the possibility of resumed post office closings. These concerns were communicated in 34 written submissions, 55 letters, and town resolutions and petitions from municipalities across the country containing 1, 309 signatures; in presentations at the public meetings by such interested parties as Rural Dignity of Canada and Solidarité Rurale; and in the findings of opinion polling and focus groups commissioned by the Review.

It is clear to the Review that meeting the needs of rural areas should be regarded as a crucial element of Canada Post's public policy responsibilities. Nearly 25% of our nation's population - a total of approximately 6.3 million Canadians - is rural, and some 2.5 million of those Canadians live in communities of less than 1,000.

For this large and important segment of the population, the local post office serves a role far beyond that of its counterparts in urban centres. The mail is a particularly important communications link for people who live in the relative isolation of rural or remote areas. No less important, however, is the role of the post office itself in those communities. It serves as a social hub, as a federal presence and, in effect, as evidence that the national government still cares about each community and its residents.

According to work conducted for the Review by Decima Research, 68% of Canadians in communities with populations of less than 10,000 view their post office as a social hub, saying that they often "meet and chat with friends and neighbours" there. Not altogether surprisingly, only 26% of people in communities of over 100,000 attribute a similar social importance to their post office - a finding that confirms Canada Post's distinctive role in rural areas.

With regard to rural post office closings, two-thirds of Canadians (67%) nation-wide agree with the proposition that "when a post office closes, the community it used to serve loses some of its identity and distinctiveness." What is even more striking is that fully 80% of Canadians in communities of 10,000 people or less are united in this view of the damage inflicted on communities by post office closings. Decima Research reports that these concerns came through very clearly in focus groups conducted for the Review:

> "In the rural groups, the prospect of their post office closing caused great consternation. In both Bay Bulls, Newfoundland and Unity, Saskatchewan, it was felt that participants' lives would be greatly inconvenienced should the local post office close. (In Iqaluit, Northwest Territories this was not a

concern, as participants were confident that their local post office would not close, as Iqaluit is a remote area).

In both Unity and Bay Bulls, this reaction was not solely related to the convenience of the post office, but also to the sentiment that the community was being stripped of all of its services. The view was, 'Please don't take anything else away!'."

Cost-cutting cannot be the sole criterion for the decisions of a public sector entity like Canada Post, whose whole reason for existing is founded on its capacity to meet public policy needs. It is a finding of this Review that maintaining its network of rural post offices is a crucial and necessary component of Canada Post's public policy responsibility to contribute to national unity and our nation's social development.

The Review also notes that the situation is quite different in large urban areas, where post offices do not play a comparable community role. In the major cities, the crucial consideration is customer convenience. The Review has not been presented with any persuasive evidence that Canada Post's practice of phasing out urban post offices in favour of a proliferation of readily-accessible franchise outlets is causing substantial problems. On the contrary, this practice appears to be combining customer convenience with cost-efficiencies for the corporation. The Review therefore regards postal franchising in communities with a population of 100,000 or more as an operational rather than a mandate matter. It has no comment on this practice beyond suggesting that Canada Post maintain full and ongoing consultation with the public in all such communities, to ensure that no problems do arise.

In addition to the issue of rural postal closings, the Review was presented with significant concerns about the quality of Canada Post's service in rural areas. In particular, there were complaints about the fact that the corporation has no delivery standards in rural areas. As well, there were complaints about service cutbacks such as reductions in the number of hours rural post offices are open.

While acknowledging that there may be some unavoidable difference between types of service provided in rural versus urban areas, the Review finds that providing needlessly inferior service to Canadians in rural areas is not consistent with Canada Post's policy commitment to universal service.

There is no readily apparent justification for the lack of *any* delivery standard in rural areas. An argument can conceivably be made that it might take a day or two longer in these areas than in the cities - though even this is not self-evident. But it is inappropriate and discriminatory for the corporation to allow itself an indefinite time to deliver the mail in rural Canada, sometimes in practice as long as a week or more for letters between neighbouring communities.

Similarly, a strategic refocussing on Canada Post's core postal responsibilities should include ensuring that other aspects of service quality, including the hours of operation of post offices, do not put rural Canadians at an undue disadvantage relative to urban residents.

It is therefore recommended:

> **18.** THAT THE GOVERNMENT INDEFINITELY EXTEND THE MORATORIUM ON RURAL POST OFFICE CLOSINGS IT HAS IMPOSED ON CANADA POST CORPORATION.

> **19.** THAT THE GOVERNMENT DIRECT CANADA POST CORPORATION TO IMPROVE, RATHER THAN FURTHER REDUCE, THE QUALITY OF SERVICE IN RURAL AREAS, AND THAT THIS IMPROVEMENT SPECIFICALLY INCLUDE THE ESTABLISHMENT OF A REASONABLE DELIVERY STANDARD FOR RURAL AREAS.

7.13 Provision of Access to Government Services

In announcing the federal moratorium on the closure of rural post offices in 1994, the then Minister Responsible for Canada Post, the Honourable David Dingwall, emphasized that the postal infrastructure thus preserved would be put to greater use. He said at the time:

> "Studies are already underway to enhance the role of the post office in delivering additional government services."[34]

The Review has found no evidence of discernible progress in this regard. In fact, even though several efforts are underway within the Government to explore ways of simplifying and improving public access to federal programs and services, the role of Canada Post has barely figured in these explorations.

There is an opportunity here that, in the opinion of the Review, should not be overlooked, particularly in rural areas. Canada Post has a total of some 7,700 retail postal outlets, approximately 4,000 of them in rural and small-town communities where they are often the only federal presence.

These retail outlets could serve an additional function as, at a minimum, access points for written or on-line information about all federal programs, and for a wide range of application forms. In more ambitious scenarios, they could process some applications and deliver some services for government departments. The corporation could also, under contractual arrangements with provincial governments, offer such services in rural communities as handling drivers' licence renewals and motor vehicle registrations, issuing hunting and fishing licences and so on. As well, in cooperation with private sector providers, Canada Post retail outlets could provide a venue for access to the information highway or for banking services.

A number of other countries make much greater use than Canada of their postal networks as distribution channels for government services. In Great Britain, government departments including the Home Office, Health, Social Services, Environment, Transport, and Defence look to the post office to deliver some of their services. The Benefits Agency in the Department of Social Services, in particular, makes extensive use of postal outlets. La Poste in France provides non-postal services in rural and remote

---

[34]Minister Responsible for Canada Post Corporation, *Policy Statement: Post Office Closures and Conversions*, House of Commons, 17 February 1994; page 1.

communities, including employment information and sale of some licences and permits. The Australian Postal Corporation provides a variety of government services, including providing and processing passport applications. The United States Postal Service has provided distribution and collection of some application forms, and is now cooperating with the government on the development of an ambitious Web Interactive Network of Government Services (WINGS).

Here in Canada, the government of New Brunswick is working with Canada Post on pilot projects to deliver provincial government programs on a "single window" basis through the corporation's retail outlets.

The Review is aware that attempting to actually deliver certain federal programs and services through Canada Post could present problems of uniformity, accountability and compliance with the Financial Administration Act. There would likely be significant resistance even to making the corporation any kind of exclusive channel for access to information about Government programs. But there is no apparent reason why it would not be appropriate to use the Canada Post retail infrastructure as at least *one element* of the Government's information and, in some instances, service delivery network. Opinion research conducted for the Review by Decima Research indicated that 61% of Canadians would support such a use of postal outlets.

It is therefore recommended:

> **20.** THAT THE GOVERNMENT GIVE PRIORITY ATTENTION TO MAXIMIZING THE USE OF CANADA POST CORPORATION AS A FEDERAL PRESENCE BY EXPLORING WAYS TO PROVIDE PROGRAM INFORMATION AND, WHERE APPROPRIATE, TO DELIVER GOVERNMENT SERVICES THROUGH THE CORPORATION'S RETAIL OUTLETS, PARTICULARLY IN RURAL AND REMOTE AREAS.

7.14 Improving Mail Delivery, Speed and Reliability

A refocussing of Canada Post on its core public policy responsibilities for mail delivery should, in the opinion of the Review, include requiring the corporation to deliver that mail with maximum speed and reliability.

There is considerable evidence that Canada Post is currently falling short in this regard. The Review is aware that the last Mandate Review, the Marchment Report of 1985, recommended that the corporation relax its delivery standards but achieve greater reliability in meeting the less ambitious standards. Canada Post has undeniably achieved the recommended relaxation. But it has clearly not, at least in the perception of the public, matched it with sufficiently improved reliability.

Opinion research conducted for the Review indicates that substantial numbers of Canadians now find our postal service slow *and* unreliable. The corporation has made it well known that it commissions regular independent testing of how well it is meeting its delivery standards, and that these tests show a very high degree of successful performance - albeit only between major urban centres, and only using perfectly addressed envelopes. But the day-to-day experience of ordinary Canadians appears to be rather different. The report to the Review by Decima Research states:

> "Results from the quantitative survey reveal two areas, namely speed of mail delivery, and the reliability of mail delivery, where the corporation appears to be falling short of consumers' service expectations. Indeed, in this latter category of reliability of mail delivery, a significant number of Canadians say they would be prepared to pay more to mail a letter for greater assurances of reliability.
>
> ...40% of respondents said that Canada Post takes longer than it should to deliver local mail; 53% said it takes longer than it should to deliver regional mail addressed to a different centre in the same province; 53% said it takes longer than it should to deliver national mail addressed to a different province. In all, 72% of respondents felt that the corporation did not measure up to their expectations in at least one of the three categories of lettermail delivery."

Focus groups also conducted for the Review by Decima Research produced a similar finding:

> "Inconsistency in the speed of mail delivery came up in every group. Participants believe the postal system is generally slow. Frequent comments were made that if speed were a factor for delivery, then the participant would automatically use a courier...A minority of participants in the groups found the postal system to be reliable...If a letter or parcel *had* to get to its destination, then participants would send it via courier."

The public perception of sub-optimal service is confirmed by Canada Post's own Coopers & Lybrand report:

> " Its standards of service are less ambitious than most other postal administrations...Australia has a next day standard for all mail, including interstate major cities (with a two day standard to distant areas). The United States has a one day standard within cities, a two day standard between major cities and a three day standard to remote areas...In contrast, Canada with its relatively straight forward east-west logistics has a two day standard within cities, a three day standard between major cities and a four day standard to distant areas."[35]

Reasons of geography and climate do not suffice, in the opinion of the Review, to justify Canada Post's lack of rigour in its service standards. We have great distances in Canada - but there are considerable distances in the United States and Australia as well. It snows in Canada - but it snows in parts of the United States too without giving rise to different delivery standards in the snowy regions, and Australia is not devoid of climate. Neither distance nor weather, in any event, can explain a standard that allows three days to get a letter from Ottawa to Montreal, or from Vancouver to Calgary. The Review notes Canada Post's argument that the current delivery standards are embedded in the design of the corporation's network. But it also notes that network designs are not immutable.

If Canada Post is to focus on its public policy role of providing core postal services, those services should be excellent. If Canadians are to pay a higher postage rate to enable the corporation to carry out its core responsibilities, they are entitled to faster and more reliable service in return.

---

[35]Coopers & Lybrand Consulting, op. cit.; pages 26-27.

And if Canada Post is to maintain sufficient mail volumes to remain viable, it must provide service fast and reliable enough not to drive customers to alternative modes of communication. As its Coopers & Lybrand report points out: "The standards of service are a major determinant of mail volumes."[36]

It is therefore recommended:

> **21.** THAT THE GOVERNMENT DIRECT CANADA POST CORPORATION TO TAKE IMMEDIATE STEPS TO BEGIN IMPROVING THE SPEED AND RELIABILITY OF MAIL DELIVERY, AND TO ATTAIN A DELIVERY STANDARD OF ONE DAY WITHIN CITIES, TWO DAYS BETWEEN MAJOR CITIES AND THREE DAYS TO MOST REMOTE AREAS BY A REASONABLE DEADLINE TO BE SET BY THE GOVERNMENT AFTER CONSULTATION WITH THE CORPORATION.

7.15 The Issue of Community Mailboxes

Canada Post's recourse to community mailboxes rather than door-to-door delivery has sparked considerable debate in recent years. The Review cannot help noting, however, that the most vociferous complaints about community mailboxes came to it not from members of the public, but from the CUPW and other unions. The Review does not doubt that this was motivated by a genuine concern for the public interest, as well as by an understandable enthusiasm for maximizing jobs for letter carriers.

It is difficult, on one hand, to see this as one of the most pressing issues facing our postal system. While there is clearly some public irritation with community mailboxes, the scale and intensity of the objections are not strikingly great, and the cost of replacing all community mailboxes with door-to-door delivery would be very high - as much as $280 million a year after initial costs of $380 million, according to Canada Post's calculations, which strike the Review as perhaps somewhat exuberant.

---

[36] Coopers & Lybrand Consulting, op. cit.; pages 26.

On the other hand, there are some issues of fairness and uniformity arising out of the fact that some people in a given community may have door-to-door delivery while their neighbours on the next street are relegated to using community mailboxes, solely because their homes were built after Canada Post's cut-off date for delivery to new developments. The costs of replacing community mailboxes with door-to-door delivery only in urban centres that already have letter carrier service would be much lower than the figure cited by Canada Post for total conversion; they would, according to the corporation, be $70 million a year after initial transition and equipment write-down costs of $130 million (which, again, may well be exaggerated). It would be appropriate for the corporation to do this, if and as resources permit, after according priority attention to improving the speed and reliability of mail service.

Of considerably greater concern are the problems that community mailboxes create for elderly and/or disabled persons, particularly in inclement weather, and the safety hazards they may pose for women accessing them at night in sometimes isolated locations.

Since the financial aspects of Canada Post's recommended strategic repositioning are intended to provide additional revenues for improvement of postal services, those incremental revenues may prove sufficient to permit gradually and partially addressing the community mailbox issue. With the exception of easing the situation for elderly and/or disabled persons and reviewing community mailbox locations from the viewpoint of women's safety, however, first priority should be given to the improvements in speed and reliability of service recommended above.

With regard to elderly and/or disabled persons who have real difficulty accessing community mailboxes, it should not be beyond the capacity of Canada Post to devise - perhaps in cooperation with CUPW - a way to provide them with exceptional door-to-door service at a manageable total cost. As well, Canada Post should review the location of community mailboxes from the point of view of safety for women, drawing on the advice and expertise of local police forces, with a view to improving lighting where appropriate and relocating any particularly isolated ones to sites with greater traffic and pedestrian flow.

It is therefore recommended:

> **22.** THAT THE GOVERNMENT DIRECT CANADA POST CORPORATION TO DEVISE AND IMPLEMENT A WAY OF PROVIDING EXCEPTIONAL DOOR-TO-DOOR MAIL DELIVERY FOR ELDERLY AND/OR DISABLED PERSONS WHO HAVE DOCUMENTED DIFFICULTY ACCESSING COMMUNITY MAILBOXES.

> **23.** THAT THE GOVERNMENT DIRECT CANADA POST CORPORATION TO REVIEW COMMUNITY MAILBOX LOCATIONS FROM THE VIEWPOINT OF WOMEN'S SAFETY WITH THE HELP AND ADVICE OF LOCAL POLICE FORCES, AND TO IMPROVE OR RELOCATE ANY THAT ARE FOUND TO BE POTENTIALLY HAZARDOUS.

> **24.** THAT THE GOVERNMENT DIRECT CANADA POST CORPORATION TO REPLACE COMMUNITY MAILBOXES WITH DOOR-TO-DOOR SERVICE IN URBAN AREAS WITH EXISTING LETTER CARRIER SERVICE, IF AND AS RESOURCES PERMIT, AFTER ACCORDING PRIORITY TO IMPROVEMENTS IN SPEED AND RELIABILITY OF DELIVERY.

7.16 Predictability in Dealing with Canada Post

A recurring theme in submissions and presentations to the Review from the business community is the difficulty of dealing with a monopoly that can change prices and mail preparation requirements at will and impose them as a fait accompli.

While changes in the basic postal rate require Cabinet approval, Canada Post has full latitude to change its discounts and incentive rates, to modify its definitions of what qualifies for various rates, and to change mail preparation requirements that business users must meet within the price structure.

The Review is persuaded that such abrupt and unilateral changes create a serious problem for companies, since they must prepare their operating budgets well in advance and significant unanticipated increases in mailing costs are disruptive. After the strategic repositioning recommended in this report, there is no apparent reason why Canada Post should not be able to plan any pricing, definition or requirement changes at least a year in advance and advise all potentially affected users accordingly.

It is therefore recommended:

> **25.** **THAT THE GOVERNMENT DIRECT CANADA POST CORPORATION, AFTER THE RECOMMENDED STRATEGIC REPOSITIONING, TO PROVIDE AT LEAST A YEAR'S ADVANCE PUBLIC NOTICE OF ANY CHANGES IN RATES, VOLUME OR INCENTIVE DISCOUNTS, DEFINITIONS, OR PREPARATION REQUIREMENTS.**

7.17 Process for Setting Exclusive Privilege Postal Rate

The Review's Terms of Reference call on it to recommend whether there should be any change in the process for setting the basic postal rate.

Any change in this rate is currently subject to Order-in-Council approval. The Review believes that this approach has worked well and should be retained. Giving Canada Post freedom to set the rates itself subject only to an inflation-linked formula, as the corporation suggests, would make no provision for ensuring that the public interest is optimally served. The only potential alternative that can be envisaged would be recourse to some form of regulatory process. For reasons detailed earlier in this report, the Review has recommended against establishing a third-party regulatory regime. It would be unlikely to produce good results, and the decisions of such a regulatory body would almost certainly be appealed to the Cabinet in any event.

The setting of the basic postage rate is ultimately a policy/political decision by its nature. The Government, by virtue of both its public policy responsibilities and its role as the shareholder and proprietor of Canada Post, is the appropriate body to make that decision through the Cabinet.

It is therefore recommended:

> **26.** **THAT THE CURRENT METHOD OF SETTING THE EXCLUSIVE PRIVILEGE POSTAGE RATE, BY ORDER-IN-COUNCIL APPROVAL, BE RETAINED.**

7.18 The Governance of Canada Post

As discussed earlier in this report, the Review has found that the management of Canada Post is subject to remarkably few controls or accountability mechanisms.

The Ministers with the responsibility for Canada Post have, to date, not had the staff resources to permit meaningful supervision of the corporation. The Government-appointed Board of Directors of Canada Post has not been in a position to exercise sufficient authority over its operations. The Crown Corporations Directorate (CCD), a joint organization of the Treasury Board Secretariat and the Department of Finance, has been given a limited role focussed on reviewing Canada Post's Corporate Plan and certain aspects of its financial operations.

Particularly in conjunction with a strategic repositioning of Canada Post to focus on its public policy responsibilities, adequate mechanisms must be put in place to ensure that all the actions and behaviours of the corporation are in fact fully consistent with the public interest.

In its presentations to the Review, Canada Post has suggested, rather surprisingly, that the solution is to establish a "postal service contract" between the Government and the corporation. As the President, Mr. Clermont, explained it at the Review's public meeting in Ottawa:

> "If, at the expiration of this contract, performance is inadequate, or if the criteria need to be reassessed, the Government would be well advised to look to another contractor."

Asked whether he is suggesting that if the Government were dissatisfied with performance under the contract, it should close the corporation down and start from scratch with someone else, Mr. Clermont agreed:

> "That would have to be considered...There are many ways of perhaps looking at this. The new contractor could be forced to take over the assets or the assets could remain the Government's assets and the postal operator pay a fee to use them, which is a model I believe that they were looking at in Argentina..."

The Review does not find this a good idea. It is of the view, rather, that an implicit "contract" already naturally exists between the senior management of Canada Post and the Government of Canada as the shareholder and proprietor of the corporation. The essential provision of this implicit contract is that senior management must run the corporation as directed by the shareholder and achieve performance satisfactory to the shareholder, or they may be replaced by new managers. The challenge, consequently, is not to devise new contracts, but merely to find ways of providing clear direction and effective supervision under the existing one.

This entails, first of all, providing the Minister Responsible for Canada Post with the capacity to fully exercise that responsibility. This should be done by establishing in the Minister's office a small unit or secretariat with sufficient staff, expertise and resources to carry out the specific task of monitoring the corporation at all times, advising the Minister on what needs to be done, and ensuring that the Minister's instructions are promptly and faithfully carried out. The costs of this unit should be charged back to the corporation, but it should have no control over its operations or budget.

Second, it is necessary that Canada Post's Board of Directors be composed solely of individuals with the expertise and the stature to effectively make an optimal contribution to the governance of a corporation of this size. As well, the Chairman and the President should be directed by the Government to ensure that the Board is provided with all information its members want and that it is fully empowered to perform its appropriate governance role.

Third, to ensure that all actions and behaviours of Canada Post as a monopoly corporation are fair to the public - defined as both individuals and companies - the Government should create the new position of Postal

Ombudsman. This Ombudsman should be appointed by the Minister or Order-in-Council for a fixed term of at least five years to ensure continuity. He or she should be entirely independent of Canada Post and have the authority and resources to investigate all complaints about the corporation, reporting the findings both to the Minister and to the public. It should be made a condition of employment for senior management of the corporation that they provide the Ombudsman with full cooperation and access to information.

Fourth, upon withdrawal from competitive activities, Canada Post need no longer be allowed to cloak itself in secrecy in the name of "commercial sensitivity." Its actions should be transparent, as befits an entity of the Government of Canada. It should therefore be made subject both to the Freedom of Information Act and to annual audit by the Auditor-General.

Finally, if Canada Post is both to withdraw from competition with the private sector and not be required to pay dividends, the Government may wish to consider whether it should be transferred back from Part II to Part I of Schedule III of the Financial Administration Act (FAA).

Subsection 3(5) of the FAA states:

> "The name of a parent Crown Corporation shall not be added to Part II of Schedule III, unless the Governor-in-Council is satisfied that (a) the corporation (i) operates in a competitive environment, (ii) is not ordinarily dependent on appropriations for operating purposes and (iii) ordinarily earns a return on equity; and (b) there is a reasonable expectation that the corporation will pay dividends."

Since it is recommended that Canada Post no longer engage in competition outside its core public policy role, not seek a commercial return on equity, and not pay dividends, there could be a strong rationale for transferring it out of Part II, to which it was only moved in 1989. This would have the advantage of subjecting the corporation to a higher degree of direct government supervision, particularly with regard to such matters as its operating budget.

The Review is aware, however, that there may be concern within the Government that moving Canada Post to Part I could be taken as a signal that the corporation was again eligible for appropriations. It is the Review's understanding that while Part II status precludes dependence on appropriations, inclusion in Part I does not automatically confer eligibility for appropriations and the Government can continue to rule them out. Nevertheless, it is appropriate that the Government itself weigh the pros and cons of a change in status.

It is therefore recommended:

> **27.** THAT THE MINISTER RESPONSIBLE FOR CANADA POST CORPORATION ACQUIRE THE MEANS TO EFFECTIVELY SUPERVISE THE CORPORATION BY ESTABLISHING IN THE MINISTER'S OFFICE A UNIT OR SECRETARIAT WITH THE STAFF, EXPERTISE AND RESOURCES TO CARRY OUT THE SPECIFIC FUNCTION OF MONITORING THE CORPORATION AT ALL TIMES, ADVISING THE MINISTER AS TO APPROPRIATE COURSES OF ACTION, AND ENSURING THAT THE MINISTER'S INSTRUCTIONS ARE PROMPTLY AND FAITHFULLY CARRIED OUT BY THE CORPORATION.

> **28.** THAT THE GOVERNMENT APPOINT TO THE BOARD OF DIRECTORS OF CANADA POST CORPORATION ONLY INDIVIDUALS WITH THE EXPERTISE AND STATURE TO BE DIRECTORS OF A SIMILAR-SIZED CORPORATION IN THE PRIVATE SECTOR, TOGETHER WITH AN UNDERSTANDING OF ITS PUBLIC POLICY ROLE, AND THAT THE GOVERNMENT DIRECT THE CHAIRMAN AND THE PRESIDENT OF THE CORPORATION TO PROVIDE THE BOARD WITH ALL REQUESTED INFORMATION AND IN ALL OTHER WAYS TO RESPECT ITS FULL GOVERNANCE ROLE.

29. THAT THE GOVERNMENT CREATE A NEW POSITION OF POSTAL OMBUDSMAN, APPOINTED FOR A FIXED TERM OF AT LEAST FIVE YEARS TO ENSURE CONTINUITY, WITH THE AUTHORITY AND RESOURCES TO INVESTIGATE ALL COMPLAINTS ABOUT CANADA POST CORPORATION AND REPORT THE FINDINGS TO THE MINISTER AND THE PUBLIC, AND THAT IT BE MADE A CONDITION OF EMPLOYMENT FOR SENIOR MANAGEMENT OF THE CORPORATION THAT THEY PROVIDE THE OMBUDSMAN WITH FULL COOPERATION AND ACCESS TO INFORMATION.

30. THAT CANADA POST CORPORATION BE MADE SUBJECT TO THE FREEDOM OF INFORMATION ACT AND TO ANNUAL AUDIT BY THE AUDITOR-GENERAL.

31. THAT THE GOVERNMENT CONSIDER THE POSSIBLE MERITS OF TRANSFERRING CANADA POST CORPORATION FROM PART II TO PART I OF SCHEDULE III OF THE FINANCIAL ADMINISTRATION ACT, TO PERMIT CLOSER SUPERVISION OF ITS ACTIVITIES.

Conclusion

Institutions, like individuals, must adapt to changing times and circumstances. Canada Post was created as a Crown corporation with a certain view of the balance it should strike between public policy responsibilities and commercial orientation. Then it was pushed under the aegis of a different government into a much more aggressive competitive stance. Now we find that the private sector has evolved to the point of being able to fully handle some of the activities in which Canada Post remains enmeshed, while the Government has developed a specific vision of the appropriate limits on public sector activity.

These circumstances alone would dictate that Canada Post must adapt.

At the same time, however, the corporation's competitive activities have given rise to an entirely understandable perception of unfairness among private sector companies of all sizes and in a variety of fields. Moreover, its financial performance in this competitive mode has been consistently disappointing. And Canadians are far from sufficiently satisfied with the speed and reliability of the core postal services that are Canada Post's fundamental reason for existing.

Accordingly - on the strength of thoughtful submissions and presentations from Canadians from all walks of life; of having sought the broadest and most open consultation that could be achieved within the available time; and of nine months of its own research and analysis - the Review has developed a set of 31 closely inter-related recommendations. These are intended to strategically reposition the corporation so that it may serve the interests of Canadians in the years ahead. It is hoped that they may be viewed as an organic whole, because cherry-picking among the recommended courses of action would be considerably less likely to produce the desired results.

It cannot realistically be expected that these recommendations will satisfy everyone; the interests at play are too genuinely disparate. Certainly it is unlikely that the corporation itself will be enthused, committed as it has become to a quite different vision. But without the kinds of changes that the current situation invites, one of the most important and visible entities of the Government of Canada will likely remain mired in growing public controversy and chronic financial underachievement. Canadians will continue to receive less than the excellent core postal services to which they should be entitled. Opportunities to improve the access of Canadians to government services will be foregone, along with an important chance to strengthen the federal presence at a time of significant challenges to national unity.

Canada's postal service, in its various incarnations, has served our nation well since its earliest days. It has the potential to make no less valuable and positive a contribution in the years ahead. These recommended changes, intended to combine pragmatism with a guiding sense of fundamental Canadian values, are proposed to help the Government direct Canada Post toward making that potential a reality.

8.1 Summary of Findings

FINDING #1: Canada Post Corporation is in no immediate financial danger. But its performance falls far short not only of a commercial rate of return, but also of an acceptable definition of breaking even. There is no basis for confidence that a continuation of the corporation's current strategic direction will produce sufficiently improved results in future years. Consequently, the current course imperils Canada Post's longer-term financial viability.

FINDING # 2: In its competitive activities with regard to unaddressed admail, courier services, and mailing centres, Canada Post Corporation is an unfair competitor in ways detrimental to private sector companies. Further, the corporation's misallocation of costs constitutes a form of cross-subsidization, whether intentional or otherwise. And its ability to leverage a network built up with public funds on the strength of a government-granted monopoly gives it a pricing advantage over competitors that is seriously unfair.

FINDING # 3: The shift to a predominantly commercial orientation in the years since 1986 has deflected Canada Post from its core public policy responsibilities and gravely distorted its corporate culture. This has produced serious and credible allegations of improper behaviors, as well as a situation in which a significant number of Canadians feel afraid of an entity of their own government.

FINDING # 4: Canada Post Corporation's strategic vision of expanding into competitive activities to supplement revenues and to protect itself against anticipated lettermail volume declines is imperfect in practice and in principle. In practice, the years of emphasis on competition have produced more distractions and problems than financial successes. In principle, Canada Post should concentrate on excellence in its core lettermail responsibilities as long as they are relevant, and be treated as a sunset industry and phased out if the time ever comes when they are no longer relevant.

FINDING # 5: Although Canada Post is owned by the Government, operates on the strength of a monopoly granted by the Government, and is perceived as a representative of the Government in its dealings with Canadians, the corporation is currently beyond any effective control by the Government. None of the authorities entrusted with supervising Canada Post currently have the resources to provide the strong ongoing supervision needed to safeguard the public interest.

8.2 Summary of Recommendations

RECOMMENDATION # 1:   That providing universality of service and uniformity of price for lettermail be regarded as integral elements of the mandate of Canada Post Corporation.

RECOMMENDATION # 2:   That in any future amendments to the Canada Post Corporation Act, the obligation to provide universal service at a uniform rate for lettermail be explicitly included as part of the corporation's mandate.

RECOMMENDATION # 3:   That the exclusive privilege of Canada Post Corporation with regard to lettermail be maintained in its current form.

RECOMMENDATION # 4:   That the Government of Canada direct Canada Post Corporation to vigorously defend the exclusive privilege by recourse to appropriate legal avenues, and that the Government provide the corporation with any necessary support in that regard.

RECOMMENDATION # 5:   That the Government reject third-party regulation as an effective approach to supervision of Canada Post Corporation.

RECOMMENDATION # 6:   That Canada Post remain a Crown corporation in the public sector, and that the option of its privatization as an entity be rejected.

RECOMMENDATION # 7:   That the Government direct Canada Post Corporation to withdraw from all competition with the private sector in areas of activity outside its core public policy responsibilities for providing postal services.

RECOMMENDATION # 8: That the Government specifically direct Canada Post Corporation to divest itself of Purolator Courier at fair market value and to withdraw from all other courier services, which are defined as services involving pick-up of the envelope or parcel from a business or residential address.

RECOMMENDATION # 9: That the Government specifically direct Canada Post Corporation to withdraw from all unaddressed admail services, with the exception of unaddressed materials from the municipal, provincial and federal levels of government and their elected members, which the corporation should continue to deliver as part of its public policy responsibilities.

RECOMMENDATION # 10: That the Government specifically direct Canada Post Corporation to withdraw from providing electronic products and services, subject to the following proviso: if the corporation identifies a specific product or service that meets a demonstrable public policy need and that the private sector is unable or unwilling to provide in a way that meets the public interest, the corporation may apply to the Government for permission to offer that electronic product or service.

RECOMMENDATION # 11: That the first-class postage rate be increased to 50 cents, and that this increase be accompanied by a commitment to further improvement of core postal services.

RECOMMENDATION # 12: That, in exchange for Canada Post Corporation's withdrawal from competition in the courier market, the courier industry be required to make a compensatory contribution to the corporation's revenues, in the form of a requirement that all courier shipments must have affixed to them a first-class postage stamp.

RECOMMENDATION # 13: That the Government explore the merits of levying a modest special tax on unaddressed admail to indirectly compensate Canada Post Corporation for revenues foregone by withdrawing from this field, and perhaps also to counter-balance negative environmental implications of unaddressed admail.

RECOMMENDATION # 14: That the Government direct Canada Post Corporation to bring its labour costs under the collective agreement into line with the realities of the contemporary Canadian workplace, through good-faith bargaining in the 1997 contract negotiations.

RECOMMENDATION # 15: That in the event of a failure of the collective bargaining process to achieve the necessary adjustments without service disruption, the Government be prepared to take appropriate action to protect the immediate public interest and ensure the long-term financial soundness of a strategically repositioned Canada Post Corporation.

RECOMMENDATION # 16: That Canada Post Corporation be mandated to operate on a break-even basis rather than pursue a commercial rate of return on equity, and that this break-even basis be defined as generating sufficient revenues to cover operating costs, appropriate capital investments, expansions and improvements of core postal services, and the setting aside of financial reserves to protect against revenue shortfalls in financially difficult years.

RECOMMENDATION # 17:   That the Government direct Canada Post Corporation to reassert its identity as part of the federal presence in all available ways, and specifically by restoring the Canadian flag insignia, (the Canada wordmark), to all its vehicles, signs, advertisements and all other places where its corporate identity is expressed.

RECOMMENDATION # 18:   That the Government indefinitely extend the moratorium on rural post office closings it has imposed on Canada Post Corporation.

RECOMMENDATION # 19:   That the Government direct Canada Post Corporation to improve, rather than further reduce, the quality of service in rural areas, and that this improvement specifically include the establishment of a reasonable delivery standard for rural areas.

RECOMMENDATION # 20:   That the Government give priority attention to maximizing the use of Canada Post Corporation as a federal presence by exploring ways to provide program information and, where appropriate, to deliver Government services through the corporation's retail outlets, particularly in rural and remote areas.

RECOMMENDATION # 21:   That the Government direct Canada Post Corporation to take immediate steps to begin improving the speed and reliability of mail delivery, and to attain a delivery standard of one day within cities, two days between major cities and three days to most remote areas by a reasonable deadline to be set by the Government after consultation with the corporation.

RECOMMENDATION # 22: That the Government direct Canada Post Corporation to devise and implement a way of providing exceptional door-to-door mail delivery for elderly and/or disabled persons who have documented difficulty accessing community mailboxes.

RECOMMENDATION # 23: That the Government direct Canada Post Corporation to review community mailbox locations from the viewpoint of women's safety with the help and advice of local police forces, and to improve or relocate any that are found to be potentially hazardous.

RECOMMENDATION # 24: That the Government direct Canada Post Corporation to replace community mailboxes with door-to-door service in urban areas with existing letter carrier service, if and as resources permit, after according priority to improvements in speed and reliability of delivery.

RECOMMENDATION # 25: That the Government direct Canada Post Corporation, after the recommended strategic repositioning, to provide at least a year's advance public notice of any changes in rates, volume or incentive discounts, definitions, or preparation requirements.

RECOMMENDATION # 26: That the current method of setting the exclusive privilege postage rate, by Order-in-Council approval, be retained.

RECOMMENDATION # 27: That the Minister Responsible for Canada Post Corporation acquire the means to effectively supervise the corporation by establishing in the Minister's office a unit or secretariat with the staff, expertise and resources to carry out the specific function of monitoring the corporation at all times, advising the Minister as to appropriate courses of action, and ensuring that the Minister's instructions are promptly and faithfully carried out by the corporation.

RECOMMENDATION # 28: That the Government appoint to the Board of Directors of Canada Post Corporation only individuals with the expertise and stature to be directors of a similar-sized corporation in the private sector, together with an understanding of its public policy role, and that the Government direct the Chairman and the President of the corporation to provide the Board with all requested information and in all other ways to respect its full governance role.

RECOMMENDATION # 29: That the Government create a new position of Postal Ombudsman, appointed for a fixed term of at least five years to ensure continuity, with the authority and resources to investigate all complaints about Canada Post Corporation and report the findings to the Minister and the public, and that it be made a condition of employment for senior management of the corporation that they provide the Ombudsman with full cooperation and access to information.

RECOMMENDATION # 30: That Canada Post Corporation be made subject to the Freedom of Information Act and to annual audit by the Auditor-General.

RECOMMENDATION # 31: That the Government consider the possible merits of transferring Canada Post Corporation from Part II to Part I of Schedule III of the Financial Administration Act, to permit closer supervision of its activities.

Appendices

Appendix A
Terms of Reference

Introduction

A review of the mandate of the Canada Post Corporation (CPC) is to be conducted on behalf of the federal government. The review will result in a report with recommendations to the Minister responsible for Canada Post Corporation. After consideration by Ministers the results of the Mandate Review will be made public. All deliberations of the Mandate Review should be conducted with the objective of providing cost-effective, quality services to the public.

The mandate review will be led by an independent chairperson and will meet its objectives through the conduct and analysis of studies and a review of written submissions by interested parties. A report with appropriate recommendations is to be submitted to the Minister responsible prior to July 31, 1996. A copy of the report will also be sent simultaneously to the Minister of Finance and the President of the Treasury Board.

Purpose of the Mandate Review

- Review the functions that CPC currently carries out and those which should be provided in the future.

- Conduct an analysis of the CPC's business lines in light of the heightened competition being experienced in many product and service areas.

- Assess the ability of CPC to adjust to market conditions and determine whether such adjustments are appropriate.

Scope of the Mandate Review

The Mandate Review will concentrate its efforts on the following:

Assessment of CPC's Functions

- What are the services currently provided by CPC, and should these be modified, relinquished or added to? Should alternative delivery mechanisms be considered?

- Should CPC be free to react to advances in technological alternatives to mail and, if so, what are the associated implications for the government, the corporation, businesses and the public?

- What are the social costs of the public policy functions assigned to the corporation and how should they be allocated among the corporation, government and users of the postal service? Are there opportunities for the government to reduce or offset these social costs by offering other government or commercial services through CPC's retail network?

♦ Are there further opportunities for partnering available to CPC?

CPC Business Activities in a Competitive Environment

♦ Should the exclusive privilege of the corporation be adjusted or discontinued?

♦ If the exclusive privilege is retained, should the process for setting rates for the exclusive privilege be changed and on what basis will rate increases be permitted in the future?

♦ Assess whether CPC should aim to generate a commercial return on equity or should it aim to operate on a break-even basis; what are the implications of these options, including the impact on letter rates?

♦ Is the exclusive privilege business being used to subsidize competitive products? What processes should be developed to satisfy the regulator, the competitors and the general public that CPC competes fairly in the marketplace?

Assessment of CPC Corporate Financial Details

♦ Carry out a comprehensive assessment of the current and expected future financial position of CPC and an analysis of past and planned productivity improvements, including a review of major cost reduction programs.

♦ What is the assessment of the financial risk associated with CPC's move into new business lines as compared with the financial consequences of failing to adapt to changes in consumer demand?

Governance

♦ The Mandate Review will make appropriate recommendations concerning the governance of the corporation including the respective roles of management, the Board of Directors and the shareholder.

Public meetings of one to two days will also be held in six Canadian cities: Vancouver, Winnipeg, Toronto, Ottawa, Montreal and Halifax. Further details regarding these meetings will be announced later.

Parties interested in being considered for participation in public meetings must first present a written submission to the Chairperson of the Review Committee. Written submissions will be available to all interested parties for any comments.

Appendix B
List of Submissions

Action Express Ltd.
Action on Waste - Alberta Environmental
 Protection
AEG Sorting Systems Ltd.
Air Canada
Air Creebec
Air Inuit
Alberta Federation of Labour
Alberta Treasury Branches
Algoma Publishers Ltd.
Alliston Press (1977) Ltd.
Anderson Consulting
Arctic Co-operatives Limited
Arrow Canadian Mailing Services
Artists Against Racism
Association canadienne des maîtres
 de postes et adjoints
Association des courriers et
 messageries du Québec
Association féminine d'éducation et
 d'action sociale
Association of Postal Officials of
 Canada - National
 - Edmonton & District Branch
Association of Rural Route Mail Couriers
 of Canada
Association des Usagers de la Langue
 Française
Avon Canada Inc
Baddeck public forum
Bangay, Alan W.
Bank of Montreal
Bank of Montreal, Aboriginal Banking
Banque Nationale du Canada
Battlefords Community Cablevision
Beautiful British Columbia
Bebb Publishing Ltd. - The Northern Pen
Bell Horizon
Bell & Howell Mail Processing Systems
Best, George
Billowes, Collin
Bloorcourt Stationery & Post

Bradford Group
British Columbia Assessment Authority
British Columbia Federation of Labour
British Columbia Government & Service
 Employees' Union
Brockbank, Michael
Brown, Louise
Bryden, John, MP Hamilton-Wentworth
Budget Delivery Ltd.
Burnabynow
Cable Regina
Caisse populaire Desjardins d'Inverness
Caisse populaire Desjardins de Notre-
 Dame des Bois
Calgary and District Labour Council
Cambridge Times
Campbell, Robert S.W.
Campbell Abbot Laser Mail
Canada Post Corporation
Canada Messenger
Canada Trust
Canada Wide Magazines &
 Communications Ltd.
Canadian Alliance for Postal Reform
Canadian Airlines International Ltd.
Canadian Auto Workers - Local 1990
Canadian Automobile Association - PQ
Canadian Bankers Association
Canadian Business Forms Association
Canadian Chamber of Commerce
Canadian Community Newspapers
 Association
Canadian Courier Association
Canadian Daily Newspaper Association
Canadian Direct Marketing Association
Canadian Federation of Agriculture
Canadian Federation of Independent
 Business
Canadian Gas Association
Canadian Imperial Bank of Commerce
Canadian Industrial Transportation
 League

Canadian Labour Congress
Canadian Magazine Publishers
    Association
Canadian Manufacturers' Association
Canadian Postmasters & Assistants
    Association - B.C. & Yukon Branch
    - Maritime Branch
    - National
Canadian Printing Industries Association
Canadian Publishers & Canadian Media
    Distributors
Canadian Transportation industry
Canadian Union of Postal Workers
    - Annapolis Valley Local
    - Banff Local
    - Breton Local # 117
    - Calgary Local
    - Courtney Local
    - Cumberland Local
    - Edmonton Local
    - Fundy Local
    - Fundy Local
    - Halifax Local
    - Hamilton Local
    - Kitchener Local
    - Labrador City Local
    - Labrador City Local
    - Labrador City Local
    - National
    - Nova Local
    - Ottawa Local
    - Quesnel Local
    - Scarborough Local
    - St. Catharines Local
    - St. John's Local
    - Thunder Bay Local # 620
    - Winnipeg Local
    - Winnipeg Local
    - Yukon Local # 852
Canadian Union of Public Employees
Canadian Utilities Limited
Canmore Leader
Cariboo Press
Carillon, The
Carleton University
Casket Printing & Publishing Co.Ltd., The
Centra Gas Ontario Inc.
Centraide du Grand Montréal

Chambre de commerce et d'industrie
    de Laval
Chambre de Commerce du Montréal
    Métropolitain
Chambre de Commerce du Québec
Chambre de Commerce régionale de
    Sainte-Foy
City of Winnipeg, The
City of Yellowknife, The
Cityview Housing Co-operative
Coalition pour le maintien du service
    postal
Coalition Urgence Rurale du Bas-St-
    Laurent
Columbia House
Communications, Energy & Paperworks
    Union of Canada
Commissioner of Official Languages
Competition Bureau, Industry Canada
Confédération des caisses populaires et
    d'économie Desjardins du Québec
Confédération des organismes de
    personnes handicapées du Québec
Confédération des syndicats nationaux
Conseil Régional de developpement de
    L'Abitibi-Témiscamingue
Conseil du Patronat du Québec
Conseil du Travail de l'Abitibi-
    Témiscamingue
Consumers Council of Canada
Consumers Gas
Contac Travel Marketing Corporation
Council of Canadians
Council of Yukon First Nations
Courier Newspapers Ltd.
Crain - Drummond Inc.
Credit Union Central of Canada
Cumberland Publishing Ltd.
D & J Enterprises
D.J. Media Enterprises Inc.
Dawson City Chamber of Commerce
De Marco, John V.
Deep River Community Association Inc.
Democracy Watch
DHL Worldwide Express
Dirks, Victor A.
Distribution G.B. Enr., Manufacturier
Distribution Restigouche Distribution

Dolphin Delivery Ltd.
Dream Smart Imagination Consultants
Easter, Wayne, MP - Malpeque
EDI Council of Canada
EDS Canada
Elmira Independent
EMS Press Ltd. - Claresholm Local Press
Entreprises Grolier
Envelope Makers Institute of Canada,The
Envelope Manufacturers Association
Environment Canada
Environment Manitoba
Facilitators, The
Fedechko, Larry
Federal Express Canada Ltd.
Fédération des ACEF du Québec
Fédération de l'Âge d'Or du Québec
Federation of Canadian Municipalities
Fédération des centres d'action bénévol
  du Québec
Fédération des Coopératives du
  Nouveau-Québec
Fédération des travailleurs et
  travailleuses de Québec
Financial Executives Institute Canada
First Air
Florida Gift Fruit Shippers Association
Flyer Services Ltd.
Foam Lake Review Ltd.
Fonderie d'Art d'Inverness Inc.
Franchise Advisory Council (Maynards -
  Your Independent Grocers)
Fraser Institute, The
Fundy Group Publications
Gard, William, E. F.I.C.S.
Geltman, Harold
General Motors of Canada Limited
Givelas, Dr. Robert, Bsc DDS
Glengarry News, The
Global Travel Centre
Gloucester Hydro
Government of the Northwest Territories
Grand Council of the Crees (of Québec)
  - Cree Regional Authority
Groombridge, Chris
Gunn, Angus M., Jr.
Hanover Post, The
Hobe, Nestor

Hockley, James S.
Hospital Employees' Union
Hudson's Bay Company
Independent Mailing Service Providers
Independent Printers Ltd., The
Indian & Northern Affairs Canada
Industrial Union of Marine &
  Shipbuilding Workers' of Canada
Information Technology Association of
  Canada
Instant Courier Service
International Post Corporation
Inuit Tapirisat of Canada
Inverness Oran, The
Investment Funds Institute, The
Investors Group
Jaremko, Beverly
Jessen, Michael
Jewish Post & News, The
John Howard Society of North Island,The
Kasabonika Lake First Nation
Kenaston Superdraft
Kentville Publishing
Keyes, Gene
Killarney Guide, The
Kootenay Advertiser, The
La Ronge Northerner, The
Labrador Inuit Association
Labrador West Status of Women Council
Lajeunesse et Lajeunesse Notaire et
  Conseillers Juridiques
Lakehead Social Planning Council -
  Community Info. & Referral Centre
Lanark Era, The
Lanigan Advisor, The
Lauzon, Theophile A.
Lavery, N. Harvey
Law & Economics Consulting Group, Inc.
Learning Partnership, The
Leblanc, Francis, M.P. - Cape Breton
  Highlands-Canso
Lee Valley Tools Ltd
Lefebvre, Réjean, député
Lighthouse Publishing Ltd.
Lippert, Randy
Livingston
Loomis Courier Service
Loughery, James

Lynden Air Freight Inc.
Municipalité Régionale de Comté
   D'Abitibi
Municipalité Régionale de Comté
   Papineau
M.S.J. Services Ltd.
M.T. Publishing Co. Ltd.
Mail Boxes Etc.
Mail Boxes Etc. Member # 157
Mailing Centres of Saskatchewan, The
Majuscule Design
Makivik Corporation
Malfern Management
Manitoba Federation of Labour
Manitoba Hydro
Manitoba Industry Action Committee
Maple Ridge-Pitt Meadows Times
Mario, Dean
Maritime Broadcasting System
Maritime-Ontario Freight Lines Limited
McEachern, Bruce G.
McKenna, The Honourable Frank
Melville Advance Publishing Co. 1986
   Ltd., The
Messageries Publi-Maison Ltée
Metroland, Printing, Publishing &
   Distributing Ltd.
Mid-North Monitor
Ministry of Environment and Energy
Ministère du Revenu, Québec
Mok, Kelvin
Monsour, Nicholas
Morgan DeLoin, Yona
Mowat Express
Municipal Electric Association
Municipalité de Saint-Clément
Musée du Bronze d'Inverness
Muskoka Delivery Service
Muskoka Publications Group Inc.
Mutual Group
NDP Caucus Office
Nanaimo, Duncan & District Labour
   Council
Nason, Doreen
National Action Committee on the
   Status of Women
National Anti-Poverty Organization
National Association of Letter Carriers

National Association of Major Mail Users
National Farmers Union
National Union of Public & General
   Employees
Net Income Stabilization Account
   Administration
Neuteboom, Catherine
New Brunswick Federation of Labour
New Brunswick Telephone Company
New Westminster & District Labour
   Council
New Zealand Post
Newfoundland & Labrador Federation
   of Labour
Newfoundland & Labrador Women's
   Institute
Newspaper Association of America
North Shore News
North West Company, The
North York Hydro
Northern Postal Service Customer
   Council
Nova Scotia Federation of Labour
Nova Scotia Government Employees
   Union
Nova Scotia League for Equal
   Opportunities
Nova Scotia Power
Nova Scotia Power
Now Community, The
Now Newspaper, Coquitlam
Office des personnes handicapées
Olson, G.C.
Ontario Motor Coach Association
Ontario Trucking Association
Orillia Water, Light & Power Commission
Ottawa Carleton Home Builders'
   Association
Ottawa Hydro
Outlook, The
Oxfam Canada
Oxford Journal, The
Pack & Post
Pak Mail
Partnership Express Inc.
Patterson, Dennis
Pearson - Shoyama Institute
Perth Courier

Peterborough Coalition for Social
  Justice
Peterborough & District Labour Council
Pharmaprix
Pitney Bowes
Placebo Point Farm
Points North Air Services Inc.
Pontiac Journal
Porte-parole des résidents du sect. # 5
Postal Service Customer Council
Postal Telegraph & Telephone Int'l
Potashville Miner-Journal, The
Prince Edward Island Action Canada
  Network
Pringle, Christopher
Pronor transport et courrier
PSAC Halifax Regional Women's
  Committee
Publishers Clearing House
Quebec Community Newspapers
  Association
Quebecor Printing Canada
Quick as a Wink Courier Service Ltd.
R Plus Industries Alberta Ltd.
Reader's Digest
Recycling Council of Ontario
Regal Greeting Gifts Inc.
Regina & District Labour Council
Regroupement des Personnes à la
  Retraite
Retail Council of Canada
Review, The
Richmond News
Rivard, Jason
Rocky Mountain Printers Ltd.
Rogers Communications Inc.
Royal Bank of Canada
Royal Bank of Canada, BC
Rural Dignity of Canada
Rural Route Mail Couriers - Surrey P.O.
S.A.D.C. des Basques
Sanford Evans Communications Ltd.
Saskatchewan Association to Protect
  Public Postal Services
Saskatchewan Association of Rural
  Municipalities, The
Saskatchewan Chamber of Commerce
Saskatchewan Federation of Labour

Saskatchewan Property Management
  Corporation
Saskatchewan Wheat Pool
Schmidt, John
Sears Canada Inc.
Selkirk
Service Employees International Union
7-Eleven Canada
Shellbrook Chronicle
Shields, Ross B.
Shoppers Drug Mart Ltd
Smithfam Ventures Ltd. - Rock Creek
  General Store
SNC - Lavalin Inc.
Solidarité Rurale
SPEC
St. Ann's Bay Development Association
St. Catherines & District Labour
  Council, Local 199
St. Joseph Printing Limited
St. Lawrence Printing Company Ltd.
Stentor Telecom Policy Inc.
Suburban Service Contractor
Surrey, City of Parks
Syndicat des Postiers du Canada
  (Section de Montréal)
  (Section locale de Québec)
  (Local de Rivière-du-Loup)
  (Section locale de Sherbrooke)
  (Section locale de Sherbrooke)
  (Section de Sorel, Local 408)
Tandem Computers
Telegdi, Andrew, M.P. Waterloo
Tempest Management Corporation
Thompson Labour Co-ordinating
  Committee
3M Canada Inc.
Thunder Bay Coalition Against Poverty
Thunder Bay & District Injured Workers
  Support Group
Thunder Bay & District Labour Council
Toronto Hydro
Toronto Trucking Association
Trade Centre Limited
Tribune Weekly Newspaper
Tucker, D. K.
Uniforms - Unicorp Inc.

Union of Postal Communications
  Employees - National
  - Atlantic Region
United Mine Workers of America
United Parcel Service Canada Ltd
United Way
Université d'Ottawa
Université de Montréal
University of Toronto
University of Calgary
University of Calgary
Valcovich, Sergio
Valleyview Valley Views
Van Net Distribution Systems Ltd.
Vancouver Board of Trade, The
Vancouver and District Labour Council
Victoria Standard, The
Videotron Ltd.

Village of Teslin
Ville de Pointe-au-Père
Ville de Senneterre
Vulcan Advocate, The
W.E. Cowley Publishing Ltd.
Wakaw Recorder, The
Warren Group, The
Westmount Press Limited
Weyburn Review, The
Whitby's Community Newspaper
Whitehorse Chamber of Commerce
Wilkins, Art
Windsor & District Labour Council
Winnipeg Labour Council
World Spectator, The
World Wide Mailers
Wrap-it-up
York University

Appendix C
Public Meeting Schedule

VANCOUVER - THURSDAY MARCH 21& 1996 MARCH 22, 1996

Beautiful British Columbia
Canada Post Corporation
Canada Wide Magazines & Communications Ltd.
Canadian Union of Postal Workers
Cariboo Press
Dolphin Delivery Ltd.
EMS Press Ltd. - Claresholm Local Press
Frasier Institute, The
Independent Mailing Service Providers
Lynden Air Freight Inc.
New Westminster & District Labour Council
North Shore News
Now Community, The
Royal Bank
Rural Route Mail Couriers of the Surrey Post Office
7-Eleven Canada
Van Net Distribution Systems Ltd.
Vancouver Board of Trade, The
    Members of the Public: Hannah, Gord   Rempel, Jake

WINNIPEG - MONDAY MARCH 25, 1996 & TUESDAY MARCH 26, 1996

Action Express Ltd.
Arctic Co-operatives Ltd.
Canada Messenger
Canada Post Corporation
Canadian Publisher & Canadian Media Distributors
Canadian Union of Postal Workers
Environment Manitoba
Jewish Post & News, The
Manitoba Federation of Labour
Manitoba Hydro
National Farmers Union
Northwest Company, The
Pack & Post
Postal Service Customer Council
Sanford Evans Communications Ltd
Winnipeg Labour Council
    Members of the Public: Saper, Max

MONTREAL - WEDNESDAY APRIL 3, 1996 & THURSDAY APRIL 4, 1996

Association canadienne des maîtres de postes et adjoints
Centraide du Grand Montréal
Confédération des caisses populaires Desjardins
Confédération des organismes de personnes handicapées du Québec
Confédération des syndicats nationaux
Crain-Drummond Inc.
Envelope Makers Institute of Canada & The Envelope Manufactures
Association
Hebdos du Québec, Les
Makivik Corporation
Messageries Publi-Maison, Les
National Association of Major Mail Users
Quebec Community Newspapers Association
Reader's Digest
Réjean Lefebvre, député de Champlain, BQ
Société canadienne des postes
Solidarité Rurale
Syndicat des Postiers du Canada
Unicorp Uniforms Inc.
    Members of the Public: Brown, Louise   Chabot, Yves
                                       Geltman, Harold   Ferron, Yvon
                                       Villeneuve, Alain

HALIFAX - TUESDAY APRIL 9, 1996 & WEDNESDAY APRIL 10, 1996

Budget Delivery
Canada Post Corporation
Canadian Auto Workers Local 1990
Canadian Postmasters & Assistants Association
Canadian Union of Postal Workers
Casket Printing & Publishing Co. Ltd., The
Industrial Union of Marine & Shipbuilding Workers of Canada
Keyes, Gene
Leblanc, Francis, M.P.
NDP Caucus - House of Assembly - Nova Scotia
Nova Scotia Federation of Labour
Nova Scotia Government Employees Union
Nova Scotia League for Equal Opportunities
Oxfam

Trade Centre Ltd.
Union of Postal Communications Employees
Victoria Standard, The
      Members of the Public: Bellefontaine, Ernest   Carvery, Irvine
                                  McInnes, Doug   Nicholson, Alison

TORONTO - WEDNESDAY APRIL 17, 1996, THURSDAY APRIL 18, 1996 & FRIDAY APRIL 19, 1996

Arrow Canadian Mailing Services
Bank of Montréal - Aboriginal Banking
Bryden, John, M.P.
Campbell Abbot Laser Mail
Canada Post Corporation
Canadian Business Forms Association
Canadian Chamber of Commerce
Canadian Daily Newspaper Association
Canadian Direct Marketing Association
Canadian Industrial Transportation League, The
Canadian Magazine Publishers
Canadian Printing Industries Association
Canadian Union of Postal Workers
Consumers Gas
DHL Worldwide Express
Elmira Independent
Financial Executives Institute Canada
Instant Courier Service
Law & Economics Consulting Group Inc./University of Toronto
Mail Boxes Etc.
Metroland Printing, Publishing and Distributing Ltd.
Mowat Express
Municipal Electric Association
Muskoka Publications Group Inc.
Ontario Trucking Association
Pak Mail
Publishers Clearing House
Recycling Council of Ontario
Rogers Communications Inc.
United Parcel Service Canada Ltd.
Whitby Free Press
      Members of the Public: Campbell, Robert   Carrol, Doug
                                  McFall, Michael   Newton, John

OTTAWA - WEDNESDAY APRIL 24, 1996, THURSDAY APRIL 25, 1996 & FRIDAY APRIL 26, 1996

Association of Postal Officials of Canada
Canada Post Corporation
Canadian Community Newspaper Association
Canadian Courier Association
Canadian Federation of Independent Business
Canadian Gas Association
Canadian Labour Congress
Canadian Postmasters & Assistants Association
Canadian Union of Postal Workers
Canadian Union of Public Employees
Competition Bureau, Industry Canada
Council of Canadians
Democracy Watch
Environment Canada
Federal Express
Franchise Advisory Council
Glengarry News
Lanark Era
Lee Valley Tools Ltd.
Ottawa Carleton Home Builders' Association
Rural Dignity of Canada
Stentor Telecom Policy Inc.
Telegdi, Andrew, M.P.
Union of Postal Communication Employees

Members of the Public:

Brodeur, Réjean	Buckmuller, Karl
Chenkie, Chris	Drake, Ron
Dogget, Steve	Flegg, John
Irons, Rick	Kelly, Patrick
McCallum, Freddi	McMillan, Nancy
Parry, Janet	El Sherif, Hisham
Whiffen, Trevor	Williams, Jeff
(two anonymous)	

Appendix D
Executive Summary of
Decima Research Report

1. Methodology

Decima Research was commissioned by the Canada Post Mandate Review to undertake a broad program of public opinion research to determine Canadians' views on postal issues. Quantitative research was based on a telephone survey of 1500 Canadians conducted from June 10 to June 12, 1996. For the qualitative portion of the research, 13 focus groups were conducted nationwide in both urban and rural/remote locations: Bay Bulls, Newfoundland (2 groups); Calgary, Alberta (2); Iqaluit, Northwest Territories (3); Montreal, Quebec (2); Toronto, Ontario (2); and Unity, Saskatchewan (2). A total of 96 individuals, selected randomly, participated in these focus groups.

2. Findings

2.1 Over-all Satisfaction Levels

On the surface, Canadians appear to be satisfied with postal service "in general". That said, results from the quantitative survey reveal two areas, namely speed of mail delivery, and the reliability of mail delivery, where the corporation appears to be falling short of consumer's service expectations. Indeed, in this latter category of reliability of mail delivery, a significant number of Canadians say they would be prepared to pay more to mail a letter for greater assurances of reliability. There is a distinct lack of intensity associated with their overall satisfaction levels. On balance, three in four Canadians (76%) said they were satisfied with postal services "in general". However only 32% said they were "very satisfied", with a further 44% saying they were only "somewhat satisfied".

There was very little variation in recorded satisfaction levels with one notable exception. The *intensity* of satisfaction levels varied significantly from west to east. Residents of British Columbia were the least likely to say they were "very satisfied" (20%), compared to residents of Quebec (41%), and Atlantic Canada (39%). Only one in four Prairie residents said they were "very satisfied", while Ontario residents came squarely down on the national average (32%).

2.2 Mail Delivery: Performance and Expectations

Despite reasonable levels of over-all satisfaction, Canada Post is not meeting Canadians' expectations for the speed of mail delivery. Respondents were asked how long they thought it would take Canada Post to deliver a letter across town, within a province, and between provinces. They were then asked how long they thought **"it should"** take Canada Post to deliver that same letter.

The results clearly suggest a distinct gap between the mail delivery expectations Canadians hold, and the results they believe Canada Post produces.

Just under one-third of Canadians (32%) thought Canada Post would deliver a letter within the same city in one day. However, 51% said they **should** be able to deliver it in one day.

Asked how long they thought it would take Canada Post to deliver a letter to a different city or town within the same province, 24% said between one to two days. Asked how long it **should** take, almost double that number, (47%), said one to two days.

Finally, asked how long it would take Canada Post to move a letter between provinces, 19% said one to three days. Again, almost double that number, (39%), believe that the Corporation **should** be able to deliver that letter in the same period of time.

This is supported by the focus group findings:

> *"So, if I wanted to send something for business, I'm not going to deal with Canada Post. When somebody needs something for the next day, I'm not going to send it by Canada Post."* - Montreal focus group.

2.3 Canada Post as a Federal Presence in Communities

Canadians are quick to acknowledge Canada Post's importance as a federal presence in their community. Indeed, just over eight in ten (82%) agreed with the proposition that *"the post office is an important federal government presence in a community".* Fully 55% "strongly agreed" with the proposition. This sentiment received strong majority support in every region, but was particularly intense in Atlantic Canada where 68% of respondents "strongly agreed" with the proposition.

> *"...all I'm saying is I'd hate to see it (the post office) go. I mean, we are forever losing something."* - Bay Bulls focus group.

Given this finding, it is not surprising that two-thirds of Canadians agreed with the proposition that "when a post office closes, the community it used to serve loses some of its identity and distinctiveness". As might be expected, agreement with that sentiment strengthens on the basis of community size. Fifty-five percent (55%) of those living in communities of 1 million people or more agreed with the statement, compared to 80% of those living in communities of 10,000 residents or less.

This sentiment was voiced by focus group participants:

> " ... it still is the hub of this community where everyone comes. If I want to see people...when I go back home, that's where I'll go at noon time, and I'll stand out and say 'hi, how are you'? I don't have to bother to go into peoples' homes, it's a lot easier to go to the post office." - Toronto focus group about a rural post office.

2.4 Performance Priorities and Willingness to Pay

In an effort to determine relative priorities and willingness to pay extra for enhanced performance, respondents were asked a set of "trade-off" questions. The results from these questions appear to suggest that consumers would prefer price stability over increased speed of letter delivery. They also suggest that a sizable minority (43%) would be prepared to pay "slightly more" for better reliability of delivery.

Results from these questions were combined in an effort to determine the consistency of consumer preferences. The results of this analysis suggest that the public is almost evenly split in terms of their preferences for enhanced postal delivery standards, and their willingness to pay for those improvements.

Just over half (53%) of Canadians would prefer to keep postal prices constant rather than to pay more for quicker delivery or increased reliability of delivery . Conversely, just under half (47%) would be prepared to pay "slightly more" for improvements to the reliability of delivery or the speed of delivery.

> "... it just makes no sense that it (price) keeps going up and services don't increase." - Calgary focus group.

2.5 Lettermail Price Sensitivity

In addition to probing Canadians regarding the extent to which they would be prepared to pay more for enhanced delivery performance, respondents were also asked a series of price sensitivity questions designed to capture a broad range of price points and related perceptions of quality and value associated with those prices. Notwithstanding the results of the "trade-off" options described above, the results from this sequence of questions suggest that Canadians are prepared to spend more to mail a letter than the forty-five cent outlay they are currently charged.

When asked what price above 45 cents would be "somewhat expensive but worth paying," one third (34%) said "50 cents". A further 15% gave responses between 51-64 cents or better. Only 25% of Canadians gave a price below 50 cents as being "somewhat expensive but worth paying".

Asked what price above 50 cents would be "so expensive that the service would not be worth paying for", one quarter (24%) gave prices between 45 and 50 cents, a further 20% gave prices from 51-60 cents and 18% said 61-99 cents. Just over one quarter (28%) gave prices from $1.00 and up.

When asked at what price they would consider mailing a letter to be "a bargain" one in five mentioned the current price.

There was very little variation in responses to these questions based on usage of the postal system.

Among those who mail an average of one to three letters per month, 36% believe 50 cents was a price "worth paying" for a stamp; among those sending four to six letters per month, 34% said 50 cents was a price worth paying, while for those mailing seven letters or more, 35% said 50 cents was "worth paying".

2.6 Reaction To a Fifty Cent Stamp

Respondents were also asked what their reaction would be "if the price of a stamp were increased to 50 cents tomorrow". Almost half (48%) said they would "accept it as inevitable and shrug it off". Only 19% said they would "object strenuously and complain" while the remaining one third said they would "object, but not go out of their way to complain about it".

Those most likely to "object strenuously" were respondents who said they did not use the postal system to mail letters, and those who also claim to be dissatisfied with the current level of postal services they receive. Just over (56%) of those who said they were "very satisfied" with postal services said they would "accept and shrug off" an increase to 50 cents, while only one third of those "very dissatisfied" said they would react in the same fashion.

2.7 Potential Impact of Price Increase on Usage

Fully two-thirds (66%) of Canadians said that if the price of a stamp were increased to 50 cents, they would continue to use the system "about the same" as they currently do. The remainder claimed they would use it less. It's clear, however, that many Canadians are already seeking alternatives to using the mail. Fully 40% said they pay credit card and utility bills at financial institutions "all of the time". A further 23% claimed they use this method of payment "most of the time". The analysis reveals that a price increase would appear to have little appreciable impact on consumers' inclination to use this method of payment more than they currently do.

The study also reveals that only 56% of Canadians say they currently pay 45 cents for a stamp. Just over one-quarter (27%) claim to pay more than this. (The focus groups indicated that some consumers, particularly in Quebec, typically factor in applicable taxes when thinking about stamp prices.) A small group (14%) claimed it cost less than 45 cents to buy a stamp.

Taken together, these data suggest that Canadians are not overly satisfied with the postal services they receive from Canada Post. This distinct lack of intense satisfaction appears to be a function of concerns related to both the speed and reliability of mail delivery. While Canadians do not appear willing to pay more for speedier delivery in and of itself, they do appear to be willing to pay more for better reliability of mail delivery.

The price threshold they appear willing to accept is a price as high as 50 cents. There is a resigned acceptance of the inevitability of such a price increase amongst half the population, followed by another one-third who indicated they would stop short of open opposition to such a plan.

"It's not like we have any options really." - Calgary focus group.

2.8 Competitive Issues

The focus groups were used to stimulate informal discussion on some of the more complex issues related to the Canadian postal system. Both competitive issues such as involvement in the courier industry and the delivery of ad mail were explored in the focus groups.

While many participants did have mixed feelings about the extent to which Canada Post should be competing with private companies, one of the underlying themes in several of the groups was that not only should Canada Post just stick to delivering the mail, but they should figure out how to get that right before diversifying.

" I think that they (Canada Post) should bear in mind that their prime objective is postal service. If they can get that right, efficient and on-time... get that right first, then okay, do the other stuff. That prime thing has got to be number one." - Iqaluit

"...the less PR the better for any purposes. Just do your job properly. You know, be there when people need you and deliver the mail efficiently. It's called being invisible. Just do the job...They should stick to mail. They have enough trouble doing that right without spreading out to other things."
- Calgary

2.9 Delivery of Ad Mail

As with the courier issues, the focus groups were used to probe issues related to Canada Post's delivery of ad mail. Similar to the results of the competitive issues discussed previously, participants had mixed views. Some participants felt that the delivery of ad mail by Canada Post would contribute to revenues, and thus keep postal workers employed, and they saw this as a good thing. On the other hand, many others did not support Canada Post's delivery of ad mail for the following reasons:

♦ participants felt it was unfair as it takes away revenue from the community newspapers;

> *"I don't think that if Canada Post got rid of this (ad mail delivery) that they would go bankrupt. So I don't think that they should stick their nose in things like that, taking all these little jobs...You think of a big big machine taking all the stuff from the little companies. Little community newspapers have a hard enough time."* - Montreal

♦ participants were concerned with the fact that Canadians may be paying indirectly (through tax dollars and services) to subsidize the delivery of ad mail; and

♦ the environmental aspect of the amount of paper used for ad mail was distressing to participants in 12 of the 13 groups.

2.10 Rural/Remote Considerations

The discussions on postal service in rural/remote locations were in line with many of the findings presented in this report. However, the specific frustration with the speed of the postal services was portrayed as being especially acute for both the business community and private individuals in rural/remote areas.

Quotes from the Iqaluit Business Focus Group:

"And, as to customer service, you're trying just to meet as good a schedule as you can...sometimes we go (to the post office) twice a day just to make

certain that we didn't miss it...the mail service has diminished in the last few years."

"Again it comes down to delivery...my Express Post coming back is not getting to me. Two and a half weeks for Express Post."

"I'd like to use Express Post more, but it just isn't express post."

"Some questions come up about the computer tracking mechanism, sometimes things have got signed off here in Iqaluit and it didn't show up in our mailbox for six days after it signed off...that's not just a single isolated case. It has happened enough that it makes you upset enough to say something about it."

2.11 Twinning

Finally, Unity was a location where the proposed "twinning" of post offices may take place. Participants in the focus groups had been informed of the twinning proposal, and were incensed and outraged. They could not understand why Canada Post would want to decrease the existing levels of service, and they felt unfairly singled out, as twinning will initially affect only selected communities.

"Just a single letter forty miles and it takes a week to get there." - Unity

"Twinning don't make sense, that's what I read in the paper. Instead of improving service, it's lowering service." - Unity

DATE DUE
